· T R O P H I E S ·

Intervention
PRACTICE BOOK
Grade 6

Harcourt

Orlando   Boston   Dallas   Chicago   San Diego

Visit *The Learning Site!*
www.harcourtschool.com

Printed in the United States of America

ISBN 0-15-326149-8

4 5 6 7 8 9 10 054 10 09 08 07 06 05

Table of Contents

© Harcourt

Fluency Builder

inventive	make	Samantha
embarrassment	well	crimson
compliment	from	stopped
quality	over	blushed
resourceful	that's	ride
shrewd	some	hoses
enterprising		June

1. Samantha / was doing well / in the BMX Club's / June ride / before her wipe-out.

2. She blushed crimson / from embarrassment.

3. "I'd ride / all the time / and work on my skills," / she said; "then you'd see / some quality riding."

4. At home, / Samantha rushed / to ask Mr. Jones / if she could make his lot / into a BMX track.

5. Five kids came over / with rakes, spades, and hoses.

6. Some adults stopped / and admired / Samantha's enterprising plan.

7. "Now / that's being resourceful; / it was shrewd / and inventive / of you to see that."

8. "Thanks / for the compliment," / she said.

Dig In and Win

Circle and write the word that best completes each sentence.

1. Last June, Pam went to _____.

   clam   bag   camp

2. There was a _____ next to her cabin.

   blade   lake   lamp

3. She put her bags in the cabin and

   went to visit Glen at the _____.

   dock   cone   clock

4. It was so hot that Pam craved a _____ in the lake.

   grin   swim   pin

5. When she got back to the dock, she _____ in.

   hole   dove   nod

6. Glen ran to put on his swim _____.

   trunks   dump   flute

7. He and Pam _____ fast toward the dock.

   shades   wave   swam

8. This June, Pam has a _____ with her at Camp Rose.

   joke   fin   pole

9. When it is time for lunch, she has _____ fish.

   five   rag   fade

10. She and her pals _____ into the fish and like it.

    brim   bite   bin

11. After lunch, they ride the _____.

    cubes   fumes   mules

12. Pam is sad when it's time to go _____.

    home   hot   camp

Dig In and Win

Complete the story map below to help you summarize "Dig In and Win." Be sure to write the events in correct order.

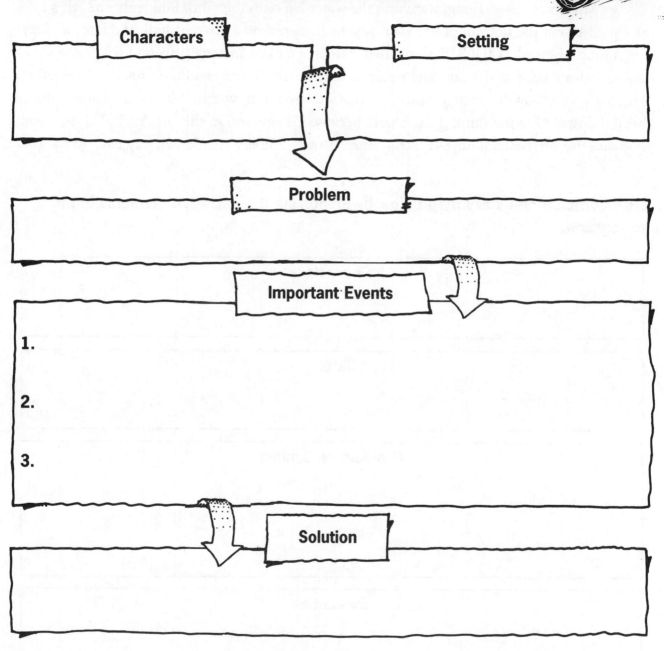

Characters

Setting

Problem

Important Events

1.

2.

3.

Solution

Now write a one-sentence summary of the story.

_____

_____

Narrative Elements

Read the paragraph.

Minerva walked along, watching the water lap onto the sand. Suddenly she felt a sharp point cut the bottom of her foot. She had stepped on a broken shell, and her foot was beginning to bleed. "OUCH!" she yelled. Minerva looked anxiously around. How was she going to walk back to the car? She panicked and started to fuss, and then finally she cried. Fussing and crying didn't help much; no one was around to watch. Then she tried to calm herself down. "Let me think. I can't walk because I'll get sand in the cut. Yuck. Maybe I could hop and use my beach umbrella like a cane." Slowly, Minerva made her way back to the car.

Now complete the story map below by identifying the narrative elements in the paragraph.

Characters

Setting

Problem or Conflict

Resolution

Harcourt

Fluency Builder

unaccompanied	not	speeding
sulkiness	your	honey
hilarious	could	best
arcade	fishing	deck
vendors	food	sell
flourish	air	meal
novelty		tea

1. Len could see Mr. Yee / on the deck, / alone / and unaccompanied.

2. Their antics / were hilarious, / but the Yees did not smile.

3. "We cannot keep this up!" / he said / with a sulkiness / that was / not like him.

4. The boat was speeding / toward the arcade / on the dock.

5. They could hear / the noise of the vendors / calling out / what they had to sell.

6. "Eat your meal / in the open air— / our food is the best!"

7. Then Len / set out / the honey cakes and tea / with a flourish.

8. It was a novelty / to eat cakes with tea / on a fishing boat.

The Tea Boat

Read the story. Draw a line under all the words that have the long *e* vowel sound spelled *ee*, *ea*, or *ey*.

     Ben planned to fix a meal for Nell and Ken. He shopped for meat, cream, leeks, and honey. "This isn't cheap!" said Ben. Then he gave the man some money. Back at home, Ben blended the cream with dill. "This will give it zest!" he said. Then he baked the meat. Nell and Ken got there at five. Ben greeted them with a grin. "We can eat as soon as I set the table," Ben said. At last the meal was over. What a treat it was! Nell and Ken said it was Ben's best meal yet!

Circle and write the word that best completes each sentence.

1. Ben invited _____ and Ken over.   **Reed**   **Chet**   **Nell**

2. He planned to make them a _____.   **meal**   **deal**   **beet**

3. He had to shop for _____.   **sweets**   **leeks**   **beets**

4. Ben spent his _____ at the shop.   **honey**   **meat**   **money**

5. Ben _____ the cream and dill.   **tended**   **blended**   **mended**

6. He had to bake the _____.   **wheat**   **seal**   **meat**

7. Ben _____ his friends with a smile.   **greeted**   **cheated**   **heated**

8. Ben's friends said it was his _____ meal yet!   **best**   **beast**   **beet**

Harcourt

The Tea Boat

Complete the story map to help you summarize "The Tea Boat."

Who are the characters?	What is the setting? Where does the story take place?

What problems do the Yees have?

What is the resolution to the Yees' problems?

Use the information in the story map to write a one-sentence summary of "The Tea Boat."

_____

_____

_____

Name _____

Prefixes, Suffixes, and Roots

Knowing the meanings of word parts can help you figure out the meanings of unfamiliar words.

➡ **Read the paragraph.**

     The famous writer stepped out of his <u>automobile</u>. His fan club was there on <u>bicycles</u>. At first the fan club had only a <u>biannual</u> newsletter. However, the writer has become so popular that the fan club now has a <u>bimonthly</u> newsletter. "Maybe my <u>autobiography</u> will make me so famous that everyone will want my <u>autograph</u>," he said.

➡ **Study the word parts to figure out the meaning of the underlined words.**

Word Parts	Language of Origin	Word Parts	Language of Origin
auto = self	Greek	*annual* = year	Latin
mobile = to move	Latin	*graph* = write	Greek
bio = life	Greek	*cycle* = circle	Greek
bi = two	Latin		

➡ **Complete the table.**

WORD	MEANING
automobile	
biannual	
bimonthly	
autobiography	
bicycle	
autograph	

➡ **Rewrite the passage, using the meanings that you figured out for the words.**

_____

_____

_____

_____

Fluency Builder

glare	around	hurt
peak	make	walk
favored	teacher	stalled
console	knew	ball
trotted	everyone	all
immune	then	
memento	set	
	found	

1. Then / I would strike out / all the team, / and everyone / would glare at me.

2. I was at my peak / and was favored to win.

3. When I hurt my leg, / friends ran / to console me.

4. I trotted / around the track / for the run-walk, / but my effort to win / had stalled.

5. When the teacher said / I should make a greater effort, / I acted / as if I were immune / and didn't care what she said.

6. I looked at my scab / and knew / it was the only / memento I had / of the President's fitness test.

7. I still play ball, / but I've found something else / I like to do, too.

8. I set my expectations / for myself, / and I am a victor / every time I do it.

Expectations

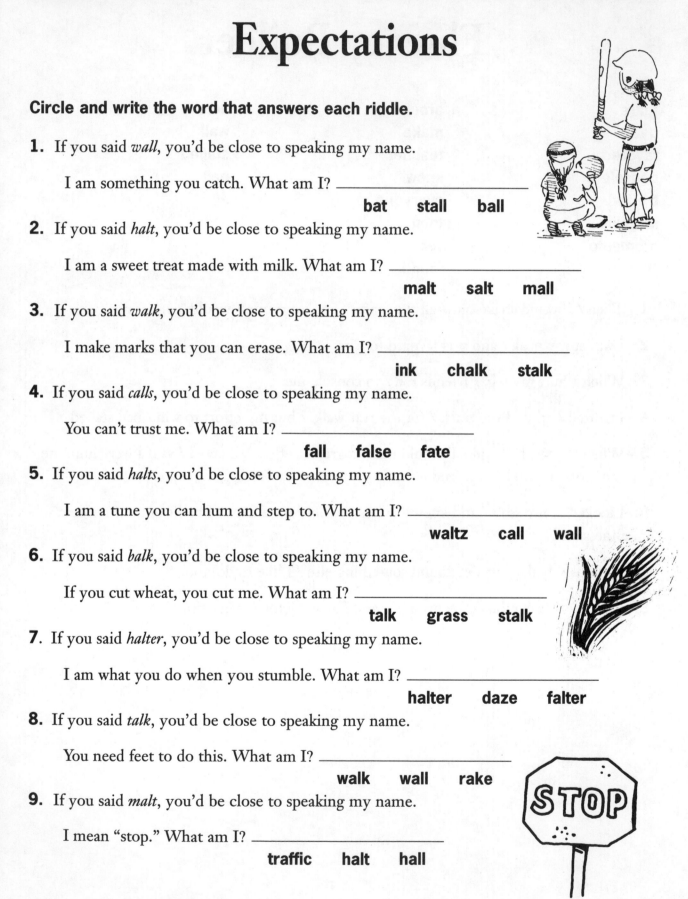

Circle and write the word that answers each riddle.

1. If you said *wall*, you'd be close to speaking my name.

I am something you catch. What am I? _____

bat   stall   ball

2. If you said *halt*, you'd be close to speaking my name.

I am a sweet treat made with milk. What am I? _____

malt   salt   mall

3. If you said *walk*, you'd be close to speaking my name.

I make marks that you can erase. What am I? _____

ink   chalk   stalk

4. If you said *calls*, you'd be close to speaking my name.

You can't trust me. What am I? _____

fall   false   fate

5. If you said *halts*, you'd be close to speaking my name.

I am a tune you can hum and step to. What am I? _____

waltz   call   wall

6. If you said *balk*, you'd be close to speaking my name.

If you cut wheat, you cut me. What am I? _____

talk   grass   stalk

7. If you said *halter*, you'd be close to speaking my name.

I am what you do when you stumble. What am I? _____

halter   daze   falter

8. If you said *talk*, you'd be close to speaking my name.

You need feet to do this. What am I? _____

walk   wall   rake

9. If you said *malt*, you'd be close to speaking my name.

I mean "stop." What am I? _____

traffic   halt   hall

Expectations

**Complete the sequence chart about "Expectations."
Write a sentence in each box. The first box has
been completed for you.**

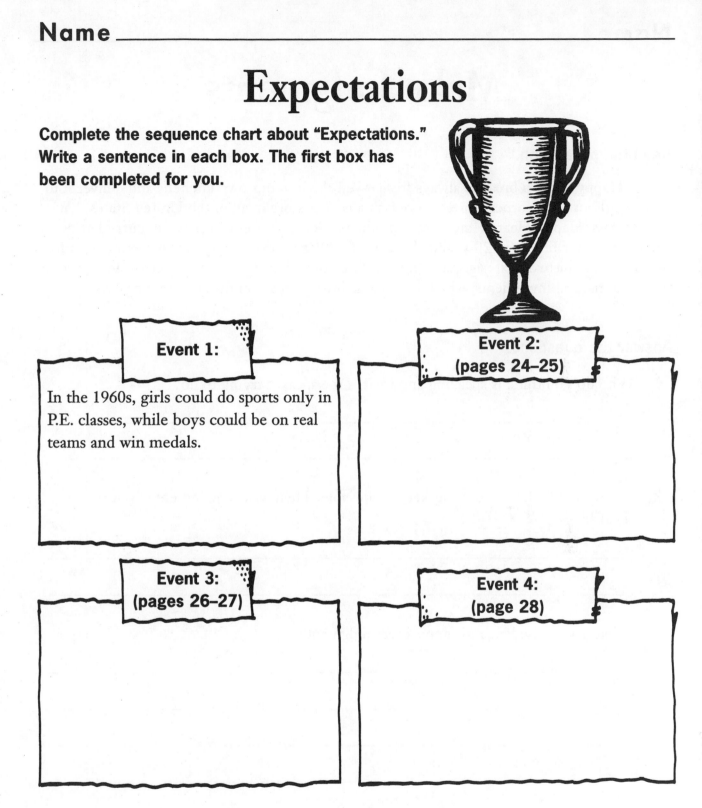

Event 1:

In the 1960s, girls could do sports only in
P.E. classes, while boys could be on real
teams and win medals.

Event 2:
(pages 24–25)

Event 3:
(pages 26–27)

Event 4:
(page 28)

Harcourt

**Now use the information from the boxes to write a one-sentence summary of
the selection.**

_____

_____

Make Judgments

Read the paragraph.

Happy Hearth bread is always fresh. We bake it in our own kitchens and deliver it to your neighborhood corner store. There isn't a corner store in all of the United States that doesn't have Happy Hearth fine bakery products. Corner stores across the country have been selling our bread for 20 years. When we first began providing your corner store with our bread, about two years ago, it sold so fast we couldn't keep it on the shelves. We use only the finest natural ingredients, which is why our bread can sit on the shelves for years.

Answer the questions.

1. Who do you think is speaking and what is the speaker trying to do?

_____

_____

2. Think about whether the speaker is believable. Then write a judgment about the speaker.

_____

_____

3. What is your evidence to support that judgment?

_____

_____

_____

_____

_____

Harcourt

Fluency Builder

reluctantly	**note**	**hard**
rummaged	**class**	**Carmen**
flexed	**went**	**stars**
instinct	**rope**	**arms**
exhaustion	**between**	**Parks**
fumed	**work**	
	line	
	just	
	friend	

1. I said / she had / an instinct / for hard work, / if not for / rope work.

2. We went at it / in our free time, / pushing ourselves / until exhaustion hit.

3. "You'll see, / Carmen— / we're going to be / the stars / of the ropes," / I said to her.

4. My friend Carmen / got in line / reluctantly.

5. Then, / with my arms and legs flexed, / I grip thc rope between my feet.

6. At the end of two weeks, / Mr. Parks rummaged in his backpack / for his notes / on our progress.

7. "For several weeks!" / the class fumed.

8. It just takes / time / and hard work.

Harcourt

The Little Big Champion

Read the story and circle the words with the /är/ sound spelled *ar*.

Clark sat in the yard with Ted. They tossed a ball to the dog over and over. "This is dull," said Clark. "Let's go to Mr. Martin's farm. I bet we can help him."

"I like Mr. Martin," said Ted. "His farm is fun, and he makes the best apple tarts!"

When they got to the farm, Mr. Martin had just parked his car by the shed.

"Hi, Mr. Martin," said Clark and Ted.

"Do you need a hand in the garden or the barn?" asked Ted.

"Well, I need to set a tarp over the garden and then clean part of the barn. Can you help with that?" he asked.

"We can," said Clark.

They walked to the garden. Mr. Martin had a green tarp. They put it over the plants. "Why is this necessary?" asked Clark, who was curious.

"I hope it will keep off the frost," said Mr. Martin. "Let's clean the barn now. Then I'll make you a fresh apple tart!"

In each group, circle the letter of the sentence that tells about the story.

1 **A** Clark wished to go to the market.
  B Clark wished to sit in the yard.
  C Clark wished to go to the farm.
  D Clark wished to start a ball team.

2 **F** He hoped to help in the garden or the barn.
  G He hoped to help wash the car.
  H He hoped to help cut the grass in the yard.
  J He hoped to help bake an apple tart.

3 **A** Ted liked the cards at Mr. Martin's farm.
  B Ted liked the tarts at Mr. Martin's farm.
  C Ted liked the car at Mr. Martin's farm.
  D Ted liked the stars at Mr. Martin's farm.

4 **F** Mr. Martin started his car.
  G Mr. Martin parked his car.
  H Mr. Martin marked his car.
  J Mr. Martin harmed his car.

5 **A** Mr. Martin asked for help setting a tarp over his plants.
  B Mr. Martin asked for help getting the car into the shed.
  C Mr. Martin asked for help getting some apples at the market.
  D Mr. Martin asked for help fixing a beam in the barn.

6 **F** The tarp will keep dust off the car.
  G The tarp will make the barn safe.
  H The tarp will keep frost off the garden.
  J The tarp will make a fresh tart.

Harcourt

Name _____

The Little Big Champion

Complete the story map below to help you summarize "The Little Big Champion."
Be sure to write the events in the correct order.

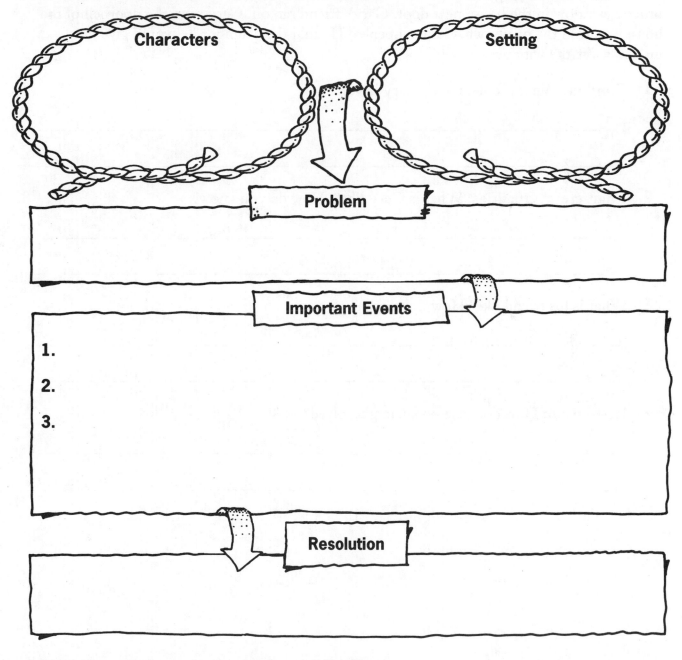

Characters

Setting

Problem

Important Events

1.

2.

3.

Resolution

Now write a one-sentence summary of the story.

_____

_____

Narrative Elements

Read the paragraph below. Then answer the questions that follow.

Gary was playing catch with a friend. He accidentally threw the ball too far and it broke a window in the house next door. Gary's friend ran off. Gary rang the doorbell of the house and told the owner what had happened. He told the neighbor he would give him money to fix the window.

1. **Conflict:** What problem does Gary have?

   _____

   _____

2. **Characters' Qualities:** What is Gary like? How do you know?

   _____

   _____

3. What is his friend like? How do you know?

   _____

   _____

4. **Resolution:** How does the problem get solved?

   _____

   _____

Fluency Builder

agenda	**went**	**way**
issue	**have**	**say**
funding	**know**	**aid**
violations	**can't**	**claim**
ordinance	**enough**	**maybe**
postpone	**you**	**explain**
effective		**afraid**

1. They went / to the Town Hall / and dug up / an ordinance— / a rule.

2. They claim / it's a violation / to have a garden / on this block.

3. Maybe / we could get / the garden issue / on the meeting's agenda.

4. You could explain / why we need / our garden and why / it is an aid.

5. They had all felt / this was an effective way / to discuss the problem.

6. I'm afraid we can't / postpone / a decision / on that.

7. Yes, / thc ordinance does say / no gardens there, / but we didn't know about it.

8. I'll donate enough land / for the lot, / so you will need / no funding for it.

Harcourt

Saving Town Garden

In each group, circle the letter of the sentence that tells about the picture.

1 **A** Nan got some mail from Spain.
   B Ray gets the mail from the box.
   C Gail finds the mail on the railing.
   D Stan's band got a big pile of fan mail.

2 **F** The train is on the plains now.
   G Gail stays on the train.
   H The plains are flat.
   J It rained in Spain today.

3 **A** Nan has some mail on her lap.
   B Nan gets the stain out.
   C The tray is in Nan's hands.
   D The tray is on Nan's lap.

4 **F** The plank is stained.
   G The plank has a crack.
   H The pan has a crack.
   J This clay is on the plank.

5 **A** The bay is windless today.
   B Ray and Gail are sailing on the bay.
   C It's raining on the bay.
   D Gail paints the bay.

6 **F** The champ failed this time.
   G The champ wins today!
   H The champ feels frail today.
   J The champ got off the train.

7 **A** The dog is wagging its tail.
   B The dog is scampering on the trail.
   C The dog drinks from a pail of water.
   D The dog takes in the mail for Ray.

Harcourt

Saving Town Garden

Complete the sequence chart about "Saving Town Garden." Write a sentence in each box. The first box has been completed for you.

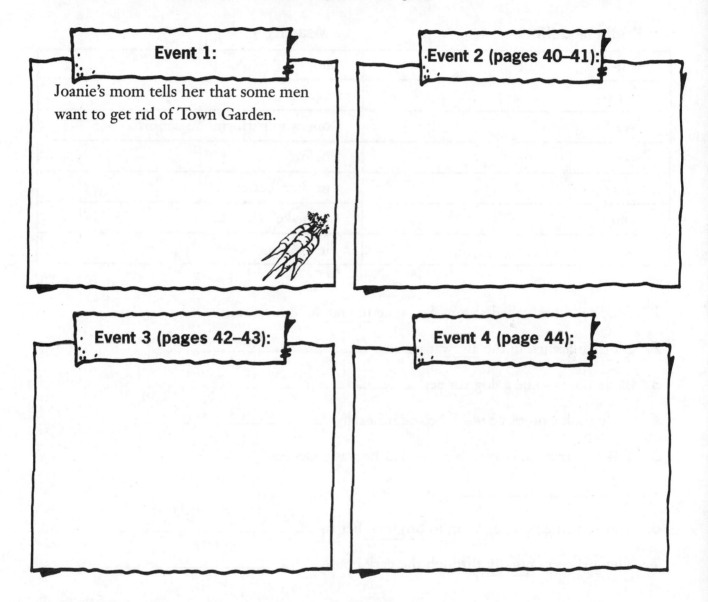

Event 1:

Joanie's mom tells her that some men want to get rid of Town Garden.

Event 2 (pages 40–41):

Event 3 (pages 42–43):

Event 4 (page 44):

Now use the information from the boxes to write a one-sentence summary of the selection.

_____

_____

_____

Harcourt

Prefixes, Suffixes, and Roots

Use the information in the chart below to determine the meanings of the underlined words.

Prefix or Suffix	Meaning
un-	not
anti-	against
-er	one who performs an action
pre-	before
out-	greater, better
-en	to make
-ly	in a certain way

1. Tony's mother yelled at him for being ungrateful. _____

2. Gloria marched in the antiwar parade. _____

3. Paula wants to be a dog trainer. _____

4. Andy took a pretest a week before his exam. _____

5. The boy tried to outrun his dog, but he was unsuccessful.

_____

6. Andrea turned on her lamp to brighten her room. _____

7. The girl crept quietly through the dark house. _____

Fluency Builder

soothingly	said	throat
occupation	was	moan
disdainfully	from	oak
exasperated	help	groan
belligerently	as	croaked
unwavering	noise	coat
	very	coaxed

1. Hearing a moan / from the oak tree / the dog growled / belligerently / at the noise.

2. Todd looked disdainfully / at the man / in the red coat.

3. With a groan / of pain / the man croaked, / "Please help me."

4. Soothingly, / Meg coaxed him / to rest.

5. Todd was exasperated / because Meg / helped the Redcoat / whose throat was hurt.

6. The men said / that hiding Redcoats was / a dangerous occupation.

7. Meg was unwavering / as she told the men / the Redcoat was very sick.

8. When the men / saw the portrait / they thought / the sick man was Pa.

Harcourt

The Portrait

Circle the words that have the long *o* vowel sound spelled *oa*. Then follow the directions.

1. Jack walks along the road. Draw the road.
2. He passes an oak tree. Put some leaves on the tree.
3. He passes a goat with no tail. Give the goat a tail.
4. Jack can see the sea from the coast road. Make some waves.
5. Add a boat floating at sea.
6. A toad sits on a rock. Make the rock.
7. Jack has a load of food with him. He needs a backpack. Make one for him.
8. As he walks, he munches on toast. Put toast in his hand.
9. "Oh, no!" groans Jack when he sees raindrops. Make the drops falling.
10. At least he has his raincoat and his umbrella. Make his umbrella.
11. Put a puddle in the road. His boots will get soaked in that puddle!
12. Add some leaves floating in the puddle.
13. Jack needs a muffler around his throat. Put a muffler on him.
14. He'll meet his goal of getting home soon. Put a smile on Jack!

Harcourt

The Portrait

Complete the sequence chart about "The Portrait." Write a sentence in each box. The first box has been completed for you.

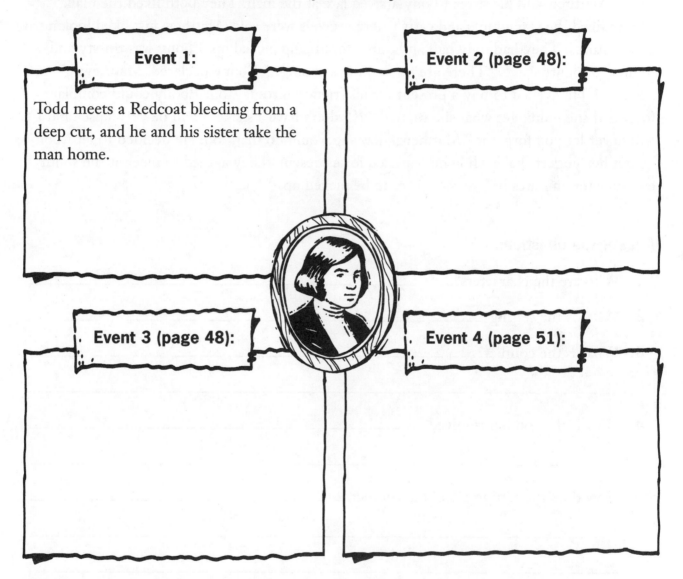

Event 1:

Todd meets a Redcoat bleeding from a deep cut, and he and his sister take the man home.

Event 2 (page 48):

Event 3 (page 48):

Event 4 (page 51):

Now use the information from the boxes to write a one-sentence summary of the selection.

_____

_____

_____

Narrative Elements: Setting

Read the paragraph.

Matthew and his sister Ebony arrived late at the mall. They both liked the mall. Ebony liked the restaurants and carts where pretzels were sold. Matthew just liked looking at all the stores. They had only half an hour before being picked up. Ebony was thirsty and wanted a yogurt shake. "There are no two ways about it," Ebony declared. Matthew hesitated. He needed to buy a present for his friend's birthday, but Ebony could complain forever if she didn't get what she wanted. "If I don't have a shake, I will be very upset and I will never let you forget it." Matthew knew she would do that, too. He decided to let Ebony go get her yogurt shake while he searched for a present. They agreed to meet at the south entrance ten minutes before they were to be picked up.

Answer the questions.

1. Who are the characters?_____

2. What is the setting?_____

3. What is the conflict?_____

   _____

4. How is the conflict resolved?_____

   _____

5. How does the setting affect the conflict?_____

   _____

   _____

Harcourt

Fluency Builder

anguish	everywhere	blowing
expanse	would	followed
engulf	early	below
compulsion	dark	window
wailed	on	growing
waver	winter	snow
disbelief	over	

1. I woke in the dark / as my dog King / wailed in anguish / below my window.

2. It was early, / but I got up / and followed King.

3. We followed Queen's familiar routine / looking everywhere / and checking each stop / she would make.

4. Snow on the ground / signaled that winter / would bring an end / to the growing season.

5. King had a compulsion / to find Queen, / and he did not waver / in his search.

6. From the hilltop, / I could see snow / blowing over the expanse / of the valley.

7. When I looked / in the vacant shed, / I gasped in disbelief.

8. I reached out / to engulf King / in a big hug.

Finding Queen

Circle and write the word that best completes each sentence.

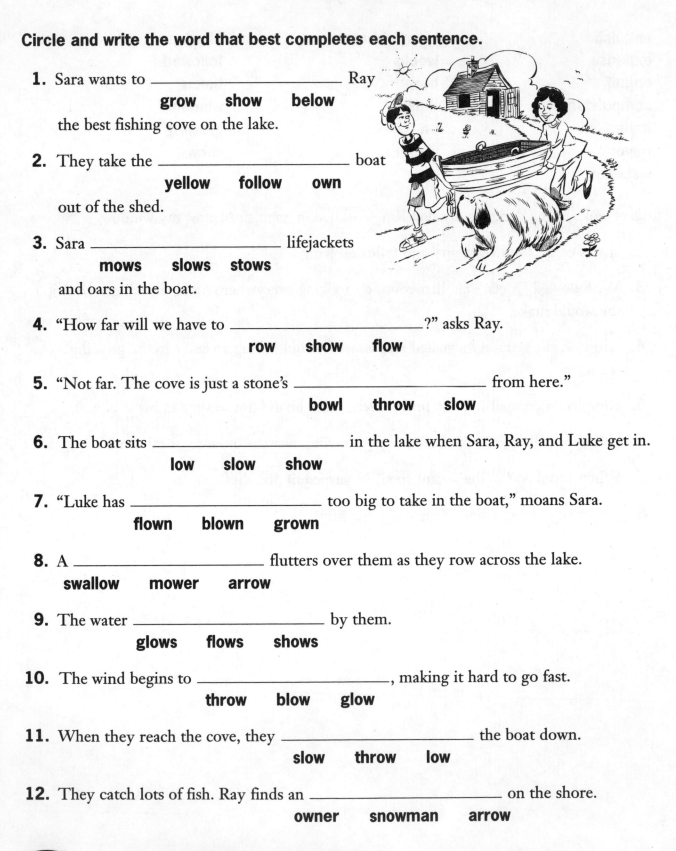

1. Sara wants to _____ Ray
   grow   show   below
   the best fishing cove on the lake.

2. They take the _____ boat
   yellow   follow   own
   out of the shed.

3. Sara _____ lifejackets
   mows   slows   stows
   and oars in the boat.

4. "How far will we have to _____?" asks Ray.
   row   show   flow

5. "Not far. The cove is just a stone's _____ from here."
   bowl   throw   slow

6. The boat sits _____ in the lake when Sara, Ray, and Luke get in.
   low   slow   show

7. "Luke has _____ too big to take in the boat," moans Sara.
   flown   blown   grown

8. A _____ flutters over them as they row across the lake.
   swallow   mower   arrow

9. The water _____ by them.
   glows   flows   shows

10. The wind begins to _____, making it hard to go fast.
    throw   blow   glow

11. When they reach the cove, they _____ the boat down.
    slow   throw   low

12. They catch lots of fish. Ray finds an _____ on the shore.
    owner   snowman   arrow

Harcourt

Name _____

Finding Queen

Complete the story map below to help you summarize
"Finding Queen." Be sure to write the events in the correct order.

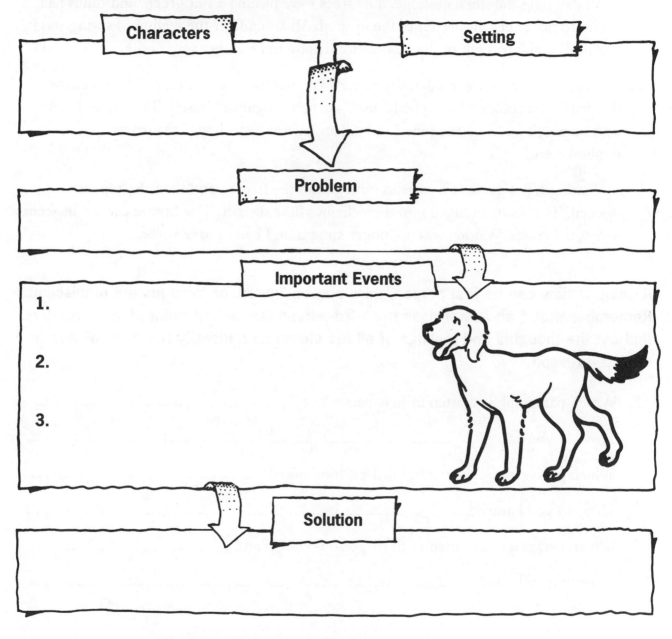

Characters

Setting

Problem

Important Events

1.

2.

3.

Solution

Now write a one-sentence summary of the story.

_____

_____

Harcourt

Literary Devices

Read the paragraphs.

A.   All day long the sun had shone. The trees were turning a soft green, and tulips had begun to poke their heads out of the ground. All around her the feeling of spring was in the air. She skipped out of the schoolyard, happy to be on her way home.

B.   As the car turned the corner, the driver's familiar hat was apparent. Adam recognized the driver. "It couldn't be anybody else," Adam thought to himself. The driver knew who he was, too. "The last time I saw Adam, he was just a boy, " the driver remembered.

C.   Waiting was a game. The carton came out of the freezer, and then the top was opened. The scoop plunged into the delicious lime sherbet. The breeze carried its scent across the room. Waiting was no longer an option; I had to have some.

A point of view can be first-person, third-person limited, or third-person omniscient. Remember that if an author uses the third-person omniscient point of view, readers find out the thoughts and feelings of all the characters. Identify the point of view in each paragraph.

1. Which paragraph is written in first-person? _____

   How do you know? _____

2. Which paragraph is written in third-person limited? _____

   How do you know? _____

3. Which paragraph is written in third-person omniscient? _____

   How do you know? _____

Harcourt

Fluency Builder

charging	down	storm
lunging	went	poor
pounced	just	corks
frantic	right	torn
yarns	could	forest
romping	hear	shore
	along	
	right	

1. Grandpa could spin / some yarns, / all right, / and we were going / to hear / one now.

2. Poor little / wet things—bobbing up and down / like corks!

3. I went charging / along the shore / of the creek, / following the branch / and looking / for a shallow spot.

4. I pounced / on that branch / and grappled with it / in the rowdy waves.

5. The possum was romping / on the grass / and went off / into the forest with them.

6. I couldn't find / a shallow part, / so I just went lunging in— / right up to my chest!

7. She was so frantic / that I just had / to do what I could / to help her.

8. During the storm, / a strong, / rowdy wind / had torn / many branches off / the trees.

Harcourt

Possum Grins

Write the word that answers each riddle.

1. My /ôr/ sound is spelled *oor*.
   You can slip on me if I am wet. What am I? _____

   floor   sort   door

2. My /ôr/ sound is spelled *or*.
   I like to run. What am I? _____

   dog   horse   born

3. Our /ôr/ sound is spelled *or*.
   Streets make us when they meet.

   What are we? _____

   corners   stops   thorns

4. My /ôr/ sound is spelled *or*.
   I'm there when you wake up. What am I? _____

   port   fog   morning

5. My /ôr/ sound is spelled *oor*.
   If I'm locked, you can't get in. What am I? _____

   door   floor   lock

6. My /ôr/ sound is spelled *or*.
   I grow on a stalk. What am I? _____

   corn   stork   torn

7. My /ôr/ sound is spelled *oor*.
   You go over me when entering your home. What am I? _____

   forest   doorstep   poor

8. My /ôr/ sound is spelled *or*.
   Drivers use me to say "Look out!" What am I? _____

   horn   storm   worn

9. My /ôr/ sound is spelled *or*.
   I can help you see in the dark. What am I? _____

   porch   formula   torch

10. My /ôr/ sound is spelled *or*.
    I'm an imaginary line around the outside of a state.

    What am I? _____

    forbid   border   north

Harcourt

Possum Grins

Name _____

Complete the sequence chart about "Possum Grins." Write a sentence in each box. The first box has been completed for you.

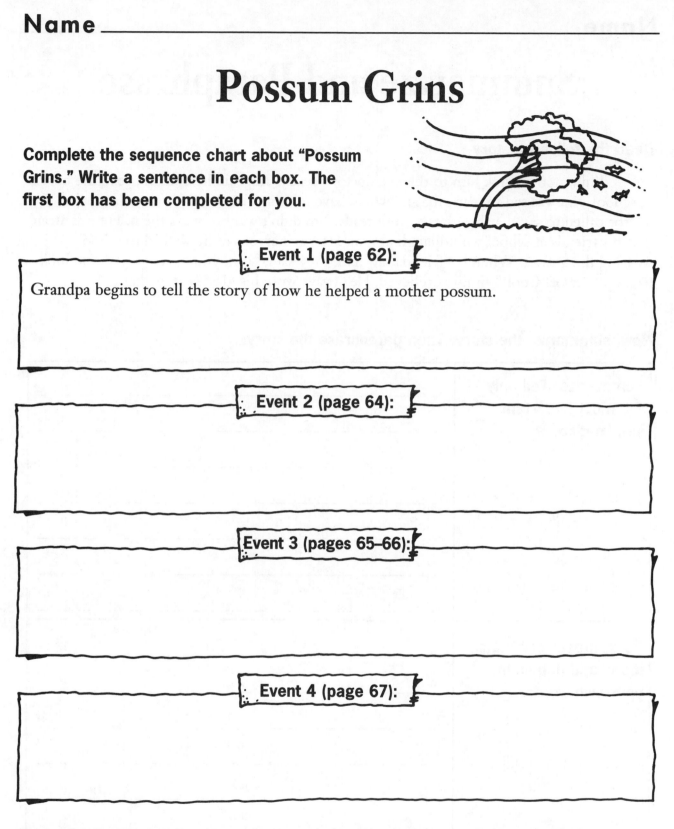

Event 1 (page 62):

Grandpa begins to tell the story of how he helped a mother possum.

Event 2 (page 64):

Event 3 (pages 65–66):

Event 4 (page 67):

Now use the information from the boxes to write a one-sentence summary of the selection.

_____

_____

Harcourt

Summarize and Paraphrase

Read the following story.

Jim's mother took him to the eye doctor because Jim said he couldn't read the board at school. Jim was sad to learn that he would have to wear glasses. A few days later, the doctor called to say that his glasses were ready. Jim didn't want to wear them. He was afraid that his friends at school would laugh at him. He was nervous as he walked to school wearing the glasses. When his friends saw him, they said, "Jim, you have glasses! You look like a professor! Cool!" Jim was relieved. He always wore his glasses after that.

Now, summarize the story. Then paraphrase the story.

Summarize: Tell only the most important information.	_____ _____ _____ _____ _____ _____
Paraphrase: Tell main ideas and details in your own words.	_____ _____ _____ _____ _____

Harcourt

Fluency Builder

impassable   down   course
grueling   find   more
perilous   trip   shore
bailed   hungry   soared
dehydration   over   aboard
rancid   would   stores
                  may
                  because

1. The course / may still be / impassable.

2. Fearing the worst, / he looked down / at the rapids / and along the shore / one more time.

3. You may find it / a grueling, / perilous trip.

4. Don soared / back over / the spot / in his floatplane.

5. He hoped / they had / bailed out.

6. He fell / through the plane door, / weak from / dehydration.

7. They were hungry / because their stores / had gone rancid.

8. They would need / to jump aboard / one of the plane's floats.

Floatplane Rescue

Read the story. Circle all the words with the same vowel sound as *shore*.

Jordan and Mortimer worked at a store. They had lots of chores to do. One day, they both ignored their chores. In a short time, they were deep asleep. Both started to snore. Just then a boar entered the store. It had sharp tusks that could be used to gore. The boar tore up many things in the store. It broke all four legs off the stand by the door. Jordan and Mortimer wore masks to get the boar out the door. Then they swore they would do their chores evermore. In the end, the store was cleaner than it had been before.

Circle and write the word that best completes each sentence.

1. Jordan and Mortimer worked in a

_____.   core   board   store

2. They always had many _____ to do.   chores   roars   cores

3. One day, they _____ their work.   poured   ignored   scored

4. They fell asleep and started to

_____.   snore   restore   bore

5. Then a _____ came into the store.   shore   boar   gourd

6. The boar _____ up the store.   porch   tore   torched

7. It broke all _____ of the stand's legs.   fourteen   four   more

8. Jordan and Mortimer _____ they
would do their chores evermore.   evermore   roar   swore

Harcourt

Floatplane Rescue

Complete the sequence chart for "Floatplane Rescue." Write a sentence or two in each box. The first box has been completed for you.

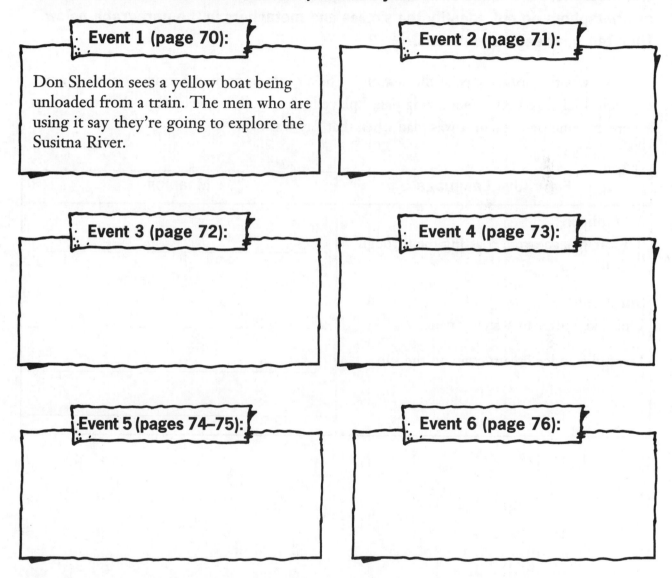

Event 1 (page 70):

Don Sheldon sees a yellow boat being unloaded from a train. The men who are using it say they're going to explore the Susitna River.

Event 2 (page 71):

Event 3 (page 72):

Event 4 (page 73):

Event 5 (pages 74–75):

Event 6 (page 76):

Now use the information from the boxes to write a one-sentence summary of the story.

_____

_____

Harcourt

Name _____

Literary Devices

Authors use figurative language to help readers imagine ideas or events. *Similes* and *metaphors* are kinds of figurative language. Similes contain the words *like* or *as*; metaphors do not. Identify the similes and metaphors in the paragraph below. Then tell what each one means.

It was the hottest day of the summer. The air was an oven, roasting me through and through. I felt like butter in a frying pan. I played outside all day, even though I was like an ice cream cone on the sun. I was glad when that day was over.

Figurative Language	Meaning
Metaphor: The air was an oven, roasting me through and through.	_____
Similes: I felt like butter in a frying pan. I was like an ice cream cone on the sun.	_____ _____ _____

Name _____

Fluency Builder

levees	just	pressure
seeping	then	swirling
floodplain	doctor	visitors
reservoirs	floor	nurses
yearned	yet	water
awed	help	earth
crested		heard

1. Water / was seeping in / under the walls and doors / and over the floor / of the barn.

2. Just then / Victor Heiser heard / a roar / that awed him.

3. The pressure of the water / was so great / that the big earth dam broke, / releasing the water / in the reservoir.

4. Johnstown lay on a floodplain, / yet the people / had not set up levees, / or walls that prevent damage during a flood.

5. When the river crested, / tons of water / came swirling into Johnstown.

6. The town suffered / a lot of damage, / and people yearned to help.

7. Clara Barton, / leader of the Red Cross, / brought fifty doctors and nurses / to help.

8. Today, / visitors to Johnstown / do not see the terrible damage / left by the worst flood ever / in the United States.

The Johnstown Flood

Read the story. Circle the words that have the /ûr/ sound spelled *er, ear, ur, or,* or *ir*. Then read each question that follows the story. Decide which is the best answer to each question. Mark the letter for that answer.

Bertha and Pearl work at their mom's pet store. The girls started helping out when they were thirteen.

Pearl is a sales clerk. The part of the job she likes best is working with customers. Pearl helps them find what they are searching for. Someone may need birdseed or earthworms.

Bertha is an expert at one thing—she can help a person pick a pet. If someone wants a pet with fur, Bertha finds the perfect dog or cat. If someone wants a small pet, she directs that person to the birds, fish, or turtles.

---

1 Where do the two sisters work?
A at a park on the corner
B at a flower stand on the corner
C at a pet store
D in the desert

2 How old were the girls when they started helping out?
F thirteen years old
G three years old
H fourteen years old
J fifteen years old

3 Which of the following is a part of Pearl's job?
A order clothes for herself
B stack crates in a corner
C work with customers
D search for her glasses

4 What is something Pearl might help a customer find?
F parts for a car
G birdseed
H a new shirt
J a purse

5 What is Bertha an expert at?
A matching pets with customers
B understanding numbers
C making fake birds
D ordering things

6 If a person wanted a small pet, what might Bertha suggest?
F a dog
G a cat
H a horse
J a bird

The Johnstown Flood

Complete the sequence chart about "The Johnstown Flood." Write one or two sentences in each box. The first box has been completed for you.

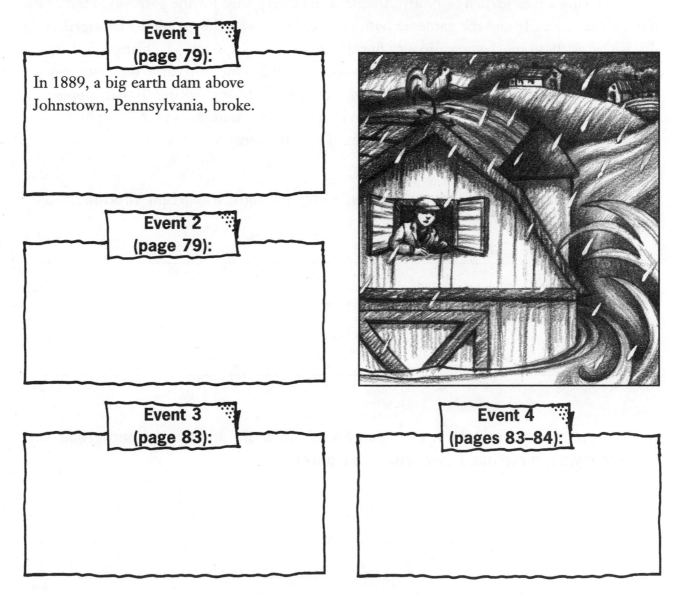

Event 1 (page 79):

In 1889, a big earth dam above Johnstown, Pennsylvania, broke.

Event 2 (page 79):

Event 3 (page 83):

Event 4 (pages 83–84):

Now use the information from the boxes to write a one-sentence summary of the story.

_____

_____

_____

Summarize and Paraphrase

Read the paragraph.

     Having a rose garden in North America can be very hard for the gardener. First of all, if a frost comes early and the gardener hasn't covered the roses, they could be damaged. A dry winter without much snow can also hurt the roses. The snow acts as a blanket. It keeps the roses warm and protects them from the wind. If spring comes too early, the roses may start to grow leaves. However, there is always a chance of a frost in spring. If that happens, the roses can be hurt again. Summer can also be a difficult season. Insects called aphids can harm buds. Gardeners and roses can have a hard time in North America.

Write a summary of the paragraph. Include only the most important information. Leave out minor details.

_____

_____

_____

_____

Now paraphrase, or restate in your own words the information in the paragraph. Use synonyms to replace key words in the paragraph.

_____

_____

_____

_____

Harcourt

Fluency Builder

astounded	flourished	secrets
reliable	animal	equipment
scouring	early	items
specialty	found	humans
newfangled	where	body
sociable	been	mummy
skewer		being

1. The Simons were astounded / to discover the body / of a man / who had died / more than 5,000 years before.

2. Carbon dating / is a reliable method for / finding out / how old an object is.

3. Scouring the site / where the mummy was found, / searchers found tools / and a copper ax blade.

4. These objects are still being looked at by experts whose specialty is studying artifacts.

5. The items / seem outdated to us, / but they may have been / newfangled / to the early humans.

6. Perhaps / he made his equipment / in a sociable group / around a campfire / while meat roasted / on a skewer.

7. The man on the ice / had a broken arm / and may have fallen / while hunting animals / that no longer flourished / in the valleys.

8. Experts believe / the Iceman has more secrets / to reveal / about his life and times.

Name _____

Iceman of the Alps

Read the story.

Eli and Eva went hiking in a remote part of the forest. Before they got very far, they could tell that they were lost.

Eli said, "I think I am going to cry."

Eva said, "Don't cry. Let's try to find our way home." A moment later, they watched a zebra go by. "Hold everything! Are there wild zebras in Ohio?" asked Eva.

"Do you mind?" the zebra asked. "I was just about to say the same thing about humans. There are plenty of zebras here. Now I must be off." Then, a python in an apron passed by.

"Don't tell me we're lunch," cried Eva.

"Luckily for you, I just had lunch," said the python. "I heated up some tasty tuna. Do you want some?"

"No, I don't think we want tuna prepared by a python," said Eva.

"What will we find next?" Eli asked.

"You'll find it's time to get up from your nap, lazy one," said Eli's mom. So he did.

Now write the word with a long vowel sound that best completes the sentence.

1. Eva and Eli went _____ in the forest.

2. Eli was about to _____.

3. Eva said they should _____ to find their way home.

4. Just then a _____ went by.

5. Eva was shocked to see a wild zebra in _____.

6. The zebra was shocked to see _____.

7. Next, a python in an _____ passed by.

8. He offered Eli and Eva some _____ for lunch.

9. Eva said _____ to the tuna.

10. Eli had been dreaming. His mom called him "_____ one."

Iceman of the Alps

Write one sentence in each box below to tell about how the Iceman was found and preserved.

Pages 86–87

Main Idea:

Pages 88–89

Main Idea:

Pages 90–91

Main Idea:

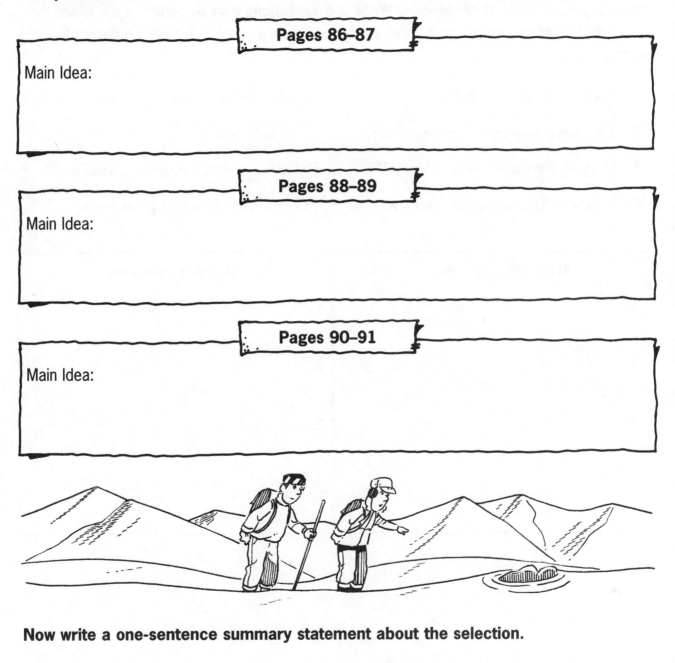

Now write a one-sentence summary statement about the selection.

_____

_____

_____

Harcourt

Text Structure: Main Idea and Details

➡ **Study each pair of sentences. Write the sentences that describe main ideas on the left side of the chart. Write the sentences that describe details on the right side of the chart.**

1. Paula wore a brown dress.   Paula was the winner of the beauty contest.

2. The mother ape gave birth to a baby.   The baby is small.

3. Martin's favorite show is "Howdy!"   Martin watches too much television.

4. Dave can lift 200 pounds over his head. Dave keeps himself in good shape.

Main Idea Sentences	Detail Sentences
1.	1.
2.	2.
3.	3.
4.	4.

Harcourt

Fluency Builder

civilization
terraces
elaborate
administrative
inhabitants
famine

where
from
could
into
world
tall
first

however
pounded
out
countless
thousands
mounds
towers

1. The inhabitants of the world / cannot be seen / from where you are.

2. When crops / could not be grown / on the terraces, / famine followed.

3. The great wall / must be both / tall and strong / to keep enemies out.

4. Some / pounded the earth / into tall mounds.

5. Before long, / the emperor's / elaborate plan / was underway.

6. Yet that tomb / saved the lives / of countless thousands more / by protecting them / from the danger / of an attack.

7. His first / administrative job / was to protect / his people / from the Mongols.

8. You can, / however, / see from the towers / some evidence / of civilization.

It's a Wonder!

Circle the words that have the same vowel sound as in *now* and *found*. Then follow the directions.

1. Howard visits the park on his birthday. Give him a crown.
2. He brings his basketball. Draw Howard bouncing a basketball on the ground.
3. He has his picnic basket. Add it on the ground next to him.
4. Stick a bone in the mouth of Howard's hound.
5. Put a mole coming out from its hole in the mound next to Howard.
6. Put a sleeping owl in the branches of the tree.
7. Add flowers under the tree.
8. Put a trout in the lake.
9. Put a mouse peeking out of its hole in the wall next to the shower.
10. Add a cat getting set to jump down on the mouse.
11. Put a flag on top of the tower in the playground.
12. Add a big cloud over the tower.
13. Put two children on the merry-go-round.
14. Add a bird to the birdhouse on top of the pole.

It's a Wonder!

Write one sentence in each box below to summarize the ideas presented on those pages about the Great Wall of China.

Pages 94–95

Main Idea:

Pages 96–97

Main Idea:

Pages 98–100

Main Idea:

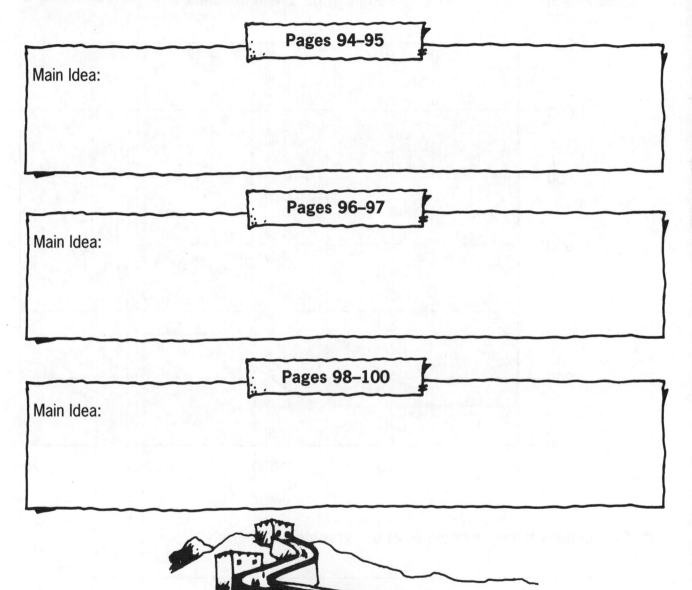

Now write a one-sentence summary of the selection.

_____

_____

Name _____

Graphic Aids

Study the graphic aid.

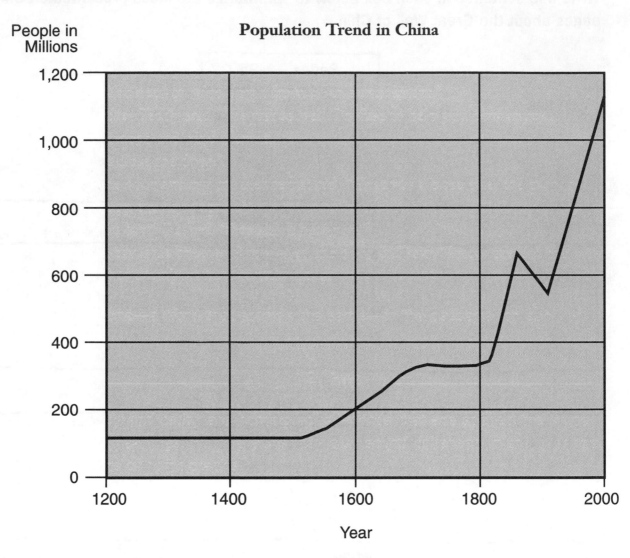

People in Millions

Population Trend in China

➡ **On the lines below, explain what the graphic aid shows.**

_____

_____

_____

What do the numbers along the left side mean? _____

_____

Harcourt

Fluency Builder

ingenious	bed	candlelight
isolated	animal	might
passageways	knew	flight
preserved	found	delighted
archaeologist	could	light
quarries	gold	sigh
	along	
	food	

1. With ingenious planning / to prevent robbery, / the tomb was cut / into the hillside.

2. Carter knew / that other tombs / at this isolated site / had been found vacant, / and so might this one.

3. The workers stumbled / upon a hidden flight / of stairs.

4. The archaeologist could see / that passageways / had been blocked up / with stones.

5. Carter / was delighted to see / piles of gold treasures / glowing in the light / of the flame.

6. In the glow of candlelight, / he saw a gold throne, / baskets of preserved food, / and a bed / shaped like an animal.

7. Carter / gave a sigh / of relief.

8. The pyramids were built / using stone from quarries / along the Nile.

Name _____

Treasures of the Pharaoh

Circle and write the word that best completes each sentence.

1. Tisha smiled with _____ when she peered
   out the window.   **bright   delight   wide**

2. The sun shone _____ on the grass outside.
   tightly   blindly   brightly

3. "This _____ will be fantastic for taking
   night   light   shine
   pictures!" Tisha said.

4. Tisha _____ Duke, and they walked
   untied   denied   frightened
   down the sidewalk.

5. They made a _____ turn and went toward
   the marsh.   **ride   mighty   right**

6. Tisha told Duke to _____ down when
   she spotted a heron.   **fight   site   lie**

7. When Duke barked, the heron sailed off

   in _____.
   time   flight   glide

8. Tisha snapped pictures until the bird flew

   out of _____.
   sight   line   fright

Name _____

Treasures of the Pharaoh

Complete the sequence chart about "Treasures of the Pharaoh." Write a sentence in each box. The first box has been completed for you.

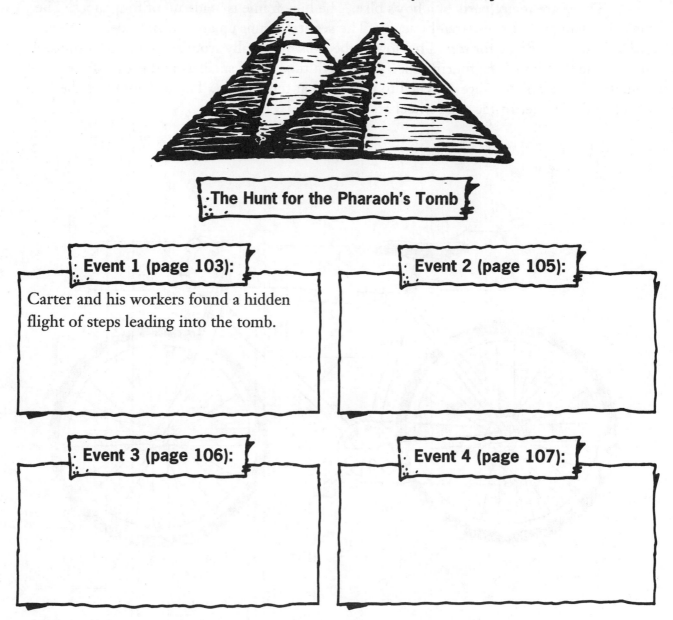

The Hunt for the Pharaoh's Tomb

Event 1 (page 103):

Carter and his workers found a hidden flight of steps leading into the tomb.

Event 2 (page 105):

Event 3 (page 106):

Event 4 (page 107):

Now use the information from the boxes to write a one-sentence summary of the selection.

_____

_____

Harcourt

Graphic Aids

Read the paragraph and then complete the diagram by labeling the parts.

There are many parts of a boy's bike. The bike frame is made up of four tubes. The top tube is a bar that runs straight across. The seat tube runs up and down under the seat. *Saddle* is another name for *seat*. The down tube runs diagonally from the bottom of the seat tube to the bottom of the fourth tube. The fourth tube is the smallest and is called the headset. The handlebars are attached to the frame at the headset. The fork attaches the front wheel to the frame. Inside each wheel are spokes.

Harcourt

Fluency Builder

provinces	sky	distances
reconstruct	used	city
aqueduct	from	sliced
mosaics	again	citizens
emblem	air	center
hygiene	like	once
	that	cinders

1. At the market / in the city center, / citizens picked up fresh figs.

2. The sky turned black, / lightning sliced the air, / and rocks, / ash, / and cinders / clattered onto houses.

3. Artifacts from Pompeii / have helped people / reconstruct what daily life was like.

4. The loaves / of bread were like / an emblem / of everyday life.

5. The large / public baths show / that the people had / high standards / for hygiene.

6. An aqueduct was used / to carry water / long distances.

7. Cities in the ancient / Roman provinces / have been covered / when volcanoes erupted.

8. People / can once again / see Pompeii's mosaics / and painted wall decorations.

Name _____

Vesuvius: A.D. 79

Read the story. Circle all the words with the /s/ sound spelled *c*.

"Greetings, citizens of Kansas City! It is time to name the winner of the Second Annual Bicycle Race. But first I will announce the prizes for first and second place." Cindy had placed second in the race. She couldn't wait to find out what prize she would get. It was hard to wait in silence when she was so excited. "The winner can celebrate her victory on the *Pacific Palace*, the biggest ship on the seven seas. This ship will take the winner and her family in a circle around the Caribbean! Second prize is a gift certificate in the amount of 750 dollars and 50 cents! The rider can redeem the certificate at any bicycle shop in the city." Cindy's face lit up. She would get a brand-new bicycle for her next race!

Circle and write the word that best completes each sentence.

1. The _____ race was in Kansas City.

    tricycle   cyclone   bicycle

2. One of the race organizers _____ the prizes.

    announced   canceled   sliced

3. Cindy finished the race in second _____.

    cellar   place   citizens

4. As she waited, she felt very _____.

    peaceful   precise   excited

5. First prize was a trip on the *Pacific* _____.

    Province   Process   Palace

6. The winner and her family will _____ her victory.

    accelerate   celebrate   certificate

7. Cindy won a gift _____.

    concert   unicycle   certificate

8. She _____ to get a new bicycle for the next race.

    danced   bounced   decided

Harcourt

Vesuvius: A.D. 79

Write one sentence in each box below to tell about the city of Pompeii.

Pages 110–112

Main Idea:

Page 113

Main Idea:

Pages 114–116

Main Idea:

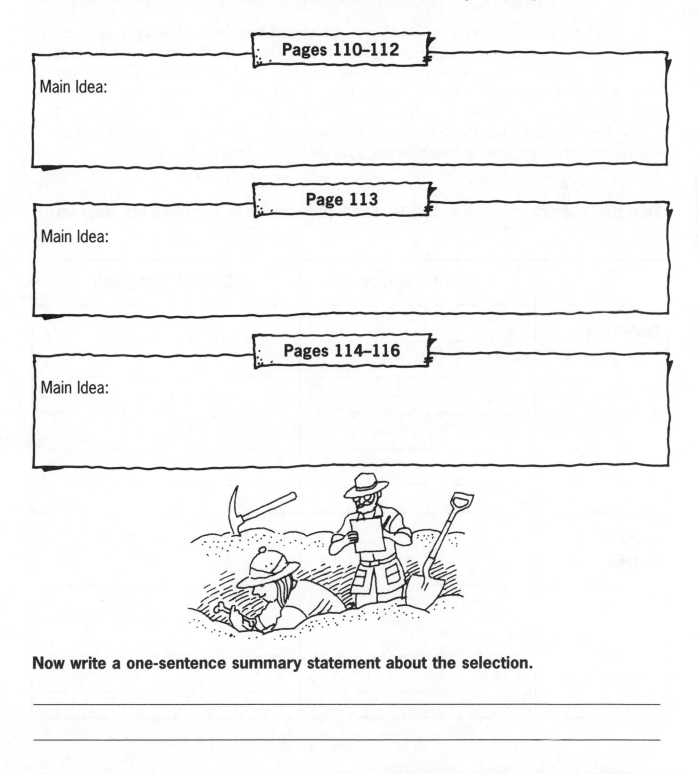

Now write a one-sentence summary statement about the selection.

_____

_____

_____

Main Idea and Details

Read the paragraphs and look for the main ideas and details.

Both men and women in ancient Egypt did a lot of hard work. Women ground grain to make flour. Women also had to weave material for clothes. Men had to harvest the crops.

Although both men and women did a lot of hard work, they were not always equal. There were Egyptian queens, but they could never have as much power as a king. Only men could hold the important offices under the king. However, women in ancient Egypt could own property. One woman owned a factory that made cloth. During one period, Egyptian women were the legal equals of men in one way: they could divorce their husband.

Write the main ideas and the details in both paragraphs to complete the diagram.

	First Paragraph	**Second Paragraph**
Main Idea	_____ _____ _____ _____ _____	_____ _____ _____ _____ _____
Supporting Details	_____ _____ _____ _____	_____ _____ _____ _____

Harcourt

Fluency Builder

disguised   who   gentlemen
democratic   think   judge
virtues   king   dangerous
brutes   good   rigid
bellowing   write   damage
rouse   they   judgment
      will   George

1. Gentlemen, / it's time we declared ourselves / independent of England!

2. And who / will write / such a document?

3. This declaration / will rouse King George / and force him / to grant us independence!

4. I, / for one, / think it's a dangerous document / disguised as a democratic one.

5. Oh / stop your bellowing, / Mr. Lee! / Who are you / to judge King George?

6. They are rigid / and stingy / brutes!

7. Are your virtues / any better, / Mr. Adams?

8. In my judgment, / it will do more damage / than good.

Name _____

The Wisdom of Jefferson

Write the word that answers each riddle.

1. I have the /j/ sound heard in *age*.
I am a very tall animal. What am I? _____
     giraffe   gerbil   gorilla

2. I have the /j/ sound heard in *generate*.
I am an indoor place where sports are played. What am I? _____
          game   region   gym

3. I have the /j/ sound heard in *wage*.
Without me, a car can't be driven. What am I? _____
          gas   gentleman   engine

4. I have the /j/ sound heard in *gypsy*.

I mean "big." What am I? _____
     grown   large   generous

5. I have the /j/ sound heard in *huge*.
You might keep a bird in me as a pet. What am I? _____
          cage   bag   gym

6. I have the /j/ sound heard in *sage*.
I am used as a flavor in a kind of soda. What am I? _____
          sugar   vegetable   ginger

7. I have the /j/ sound heard in *genius*.
You'll find several of me in any story you read. What am I? _____
          originality   page   program

8. I have the /j/ sound heard in *bridge*.
I mean "a little push." What am I? _____
     nudge   nag   gentle

9. I have the /j/ sound heard in *danger*.
I am the study of the earth's surface. What am I? _____
          oxygen   geography   gravity

10. I have the /j/ sound heard in *strange*.
I describe something that is real, not fake. What am I? _____
          grand   gemstone   genuine

Harcourt

The Wisdom of Jefferson

Complete the sequence chart about "The Wisdom of Jefferson." Write a sentence in each box. The first box has been completed for you.

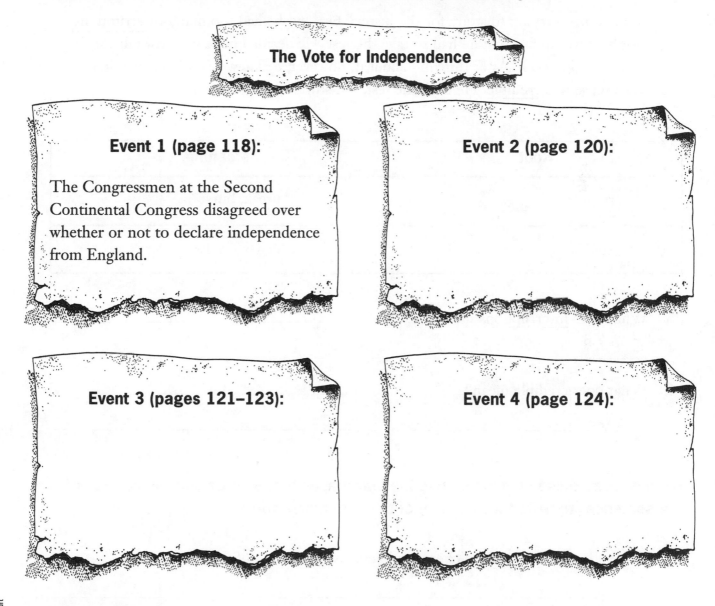

The Vote for Independence

Event 1 (page 118):

The Congressmen at the Second Continental Congress disagreed over whether or not to declare independence from England.

Event 2 (page 120):

Event 3 (pages 121–123):

Event 4 (page 124):

Now use the information from the boxes to write a one-sentence summary of the play.

_____

_____

_____

Prefixes, Suffixes, and Roots

Read the paragraph below. Decide what the underlined words mean. Use the chart to help you.

Jim had been trying to study for the history test, but he had too many <u>interruptions</u>. He thought it was unfair that he had to take the test. He decided he would just tell Mr. Carter he wouldn't do it. After thinking about it, however, he knew Mr. Carter would not think his excuse was <u>credible</u>. He took the test, but still thought it was unfair.

Root	Meaning
rupt	"break, burst"
cred	"believe"

1. What does <u>interruptions</u> mean? _____

_____

2. What does <u>credible</u> mean? _____

_____

➡ **Now read these sentences. Use the information in the chart and the context of the sentence, to write the meaning of the underlined words.**

1. The audience <u>erupted</u> into cheers and applause at the end of the play. _____

_____

2. The members of the animal lovers' club wrote a <u>creed</u>, which would be recited at each

meeting. _____

_____

Harcourt

Name _____

Fluency Builder

remote	squirrel	voice
migration	first	Joy
discouraging	along	point
nourishing	from	noise
edible	old	Leroy's
foundation	past	oyster
cavity		choice

1. We were seated on sun-warmed boulders, / feet dangling, / in a remote clearing / surrounded by a dense forest.

2. "It's migration time!" / Joy said / in a soft voice.

3. This discouraging piece of news / made me sigh, / too.

4. "I need something / more nourishing / than those, / but I guess / I don't have much choice."

5. They're from / Uncle Leroy's / berry patch, / and they're perfectly edible.

6. First we had followed a road / of crushed oyster shells along / the rocky shore / past an old lighthouse / with a cracked foundation.

7. A squirrel / stuck its head / out of a dark cavity / in a tree.

8. Just at that point / I heard / a remote honking noise.

Name _____

Follow the Wild Geese

Circle the letter in front of the sentence that tells about the picture.

1 **A** Ann and Roy enjoy the game.
   B Roy and Jeff join the game.
   C The game was spoiled by rain.
   D They played a game with coins.

2 **F** Three boys go for a walk.
   G The soil is too wet for a walk.
   H The walk was spoiled by the storm.
   J Jeff joins them for a walk.

3 **A** The soil is dry now.
   B The soil is slippery from the rain.
   C He avoids the wet soil.
   D Roy gets some soil for his garden.

4 **F** Jeff cannot avoid the oysters in the pond.
   G Roy is annoyed by the bad throw.
   H The boys avoid the pond.
   J The pond is filled with oysters.

5 **A** Jeff barely avoided the bad throw.
   B Jeff enjoyed the joke.
   C Jeff's shirt was soiled when he fell.
   D The toy landed in damp soil.

6 **F** Jeff enjoyed the game a lot.
   G Jeff feels loyal to his pals.
   H Jeff was annoyed at the rain.
   J Jeff is annoyed with Roy.

7 **A** "Don't spoil the game, boys!"
   B "Don't soil that toy, boys!"
   C "Let's join a club, boys!"
   D "Clean up that oil, boys!"

8 **F** They avoid falling.
   G They play a joint game of catch.
   H They make noise and wake the baby.
   J They catch a pointed toy.

Harcourt

Name _____

Follow the Wild Geese

Complete the story map below to help you summarize "Follow the Wild Geese." Be sure to write the events in the correct order.

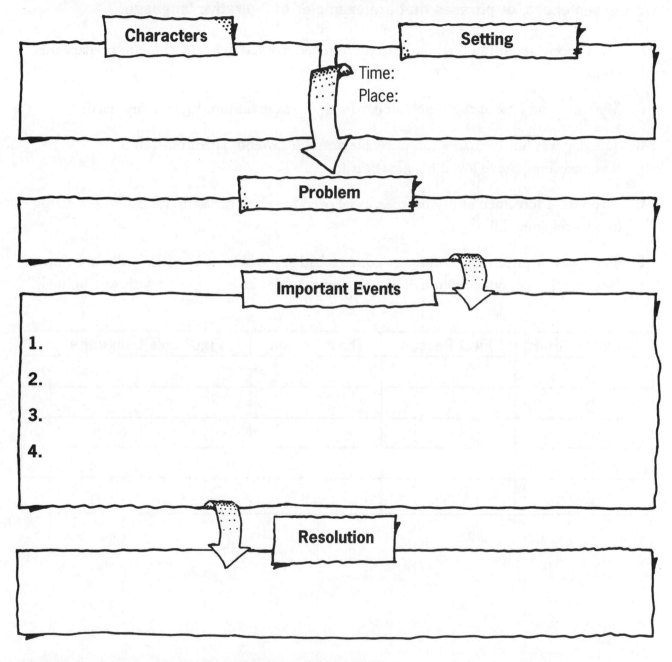

Characters

Setting

Time:
Place:

Problem

Important Events

1.

2.

3.

4.

Resolution

Now write a one-sentence summary of the story.

_____

_____

Name _____

Literary Devices

Read each group of sentences. Decide whether they are in first-person or third-person point of view. Put a mark in the correct column on the chart. Then list words, sentences, or phrases that are examples of figurative language.

A. I was happy about my birthday party. Mom had worked like a machine to prepare the house.

B. My sister and I sat at the beach all day long. It was great fun. I felt sunny inside.

C. The day was hotter than a campfire. Steve and his friends spent most of it skateboarding. Steve loved his new board.

D. "Stop it!" I screamed at my brother, as he tried to splash me with water. "You're acting like a wild animal."

E. Tyler was surprised. He had never gotten a bad grade before. His father would be upset. Just then his father came home. Tyler's stomach felt like it was filled with wild animals.

Sentence Group	First Person	Third Person	Figurative Language
A			
B			
C			
D			
E			

Fluency Builder

presentation   hard   Audrey
lilting   first   applause
melodious   knew   saw
legacy   could   audition
persevered   around   audience
flawless   music
think
family
their

1. Was your audition flawless, / Audrey?

2. I think / my family's / musical legacy / has stopped with me.

3. Their sounds / were so / melodious.

4. I sat still / and soaked up / the lilting presentation / of the music makers around me.

5. Night music, / I saw, / was pleasant and melodious / in its own way.

6. The rest of my family / have various musical talents / that bring them applause.

7. As the audience / awaited my performance, / I knew I could do it.

8. "The piano / was hard / for me at first," / Mom confessed, / "but I persevered."

Music in the Air

Read the story, and circle all the words that have the /ô/ sound spelled *aw*, *au*, or *augh*.

One day at dawn, Saul took his three daughters for a walk in the woods. Each of them was looking for something to draw. Pauline saw a hawk sitting in a tree. "I'll draw the hawk," she said. But as she got out her pens and paper, it launched into the air.

They walked farther. Taunya saw a fawn through some trees. "I'll draw the fawn," she said. But as soon as she sat down on a log to draw, the fawn was gone.

"I am starting to see a flaw in our plan," Saul said. "I taught you *how* to draw, but I never taught you *what* to draw." Saul saw his youngest daughter, Paula, sitting on the ground. "What are you doing, Paula?"

"I'm drawing some straw," she said. "It may not be very interesting, but at least I know it's not going to move." As soon as she said that, the wind came up and lifted the straw away.

Saul waved his daughters toward home. "Come on. Let's just sit on the porch and draw the lawn."

Now write the word you circled that best completes each sentence.

1. Saul and his daughters went for a walk at _____.

2. They were looking for things to _____.

3. Pauline saw a _____ in a tree.

4. Taunya spotted a _____ through the trees.

5. When the fawn ran off, Saul said their plan had a _____.

6. He had _____ the girls *how* to draw but not *what* to draw.

7. Paula was drawing some _____, but the wind blew it away.

8. Saul decided they should all go home and draw the _____.

Harcourt

Name_____

Music in the Air

Complete the story map below to summarize "Music in the Air." Be sure to write the events in the correct order.

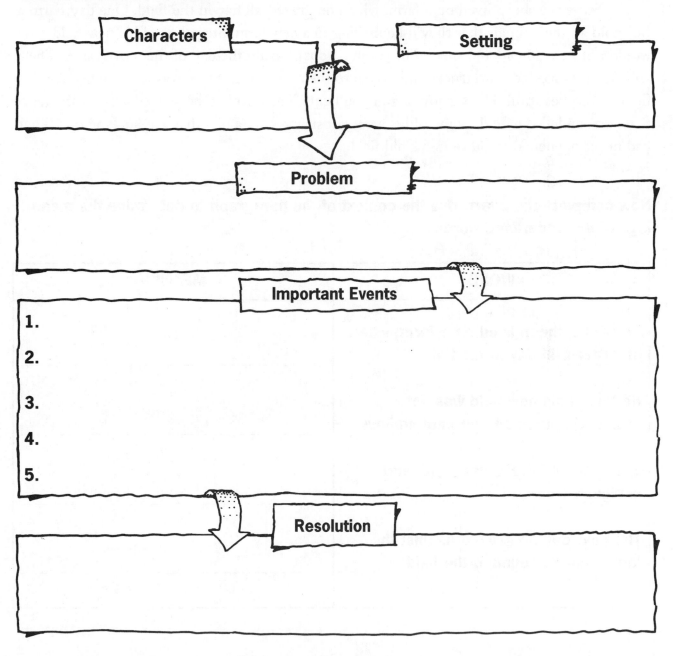

Characters

Setting

Problem

Important Events

1.

2.

3.

4.

5.

Resolution

Now write a one-sentence summary of the story.

_____

_____

Name_____

Word Relationships

Read the paragraphs. Pay attention to the underlined words.

     Steve the sheep lived on a farm, where he <u>grazed</u> all day in the field. One day Farmer Bob told all the animals that they'd be moving to a new farm. Steve hoped his new field would not be cramped and small, but <u>commodious</u>. Finally the day of the move came. The animals were loaded onto trucks and driven to their new farm. Steve was led into his new field. It was beautiful. He was joyful and <u>ebullient</u>. The next day he <u>grazed</u> against the fence that surrounded the field. Some of his wool got snagged on a nail that was sticking out. That had never happened to Steve in his old field.

Now complete the chart. Use the context of the paragraph to determine the meanings of the underlined words.

WORD	MEANING
Steve the sheep lived on a farm, where he <u>grazed</u> all day in the field.	
He hoped his new field was not cramped and small, but <u>commodious</u>.	
It was beautiful. He was joyful and <u>ebullient</u>.	
The next day he <u>grazed</u> against the fence that surrounded the field.	

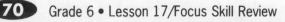

Fluency Builder

acknowledged	surprise	could
ingenuity	that	would
inquiries	store	cookies
initial	one	looked
milestone	tried	good
persistence	different	took
	work	
	things	

1. Inventors have acknowledged / that it could take persistence / and ingenuity / to work out the details.

2. Things looked bad / for the growers.

3. One farmer tried the dried grapes, / and they tasted good.

4. Soon other stores were making inquiries / about raisins.

5. He began cooking / some different ingredients / in a big kettle.

6. He had not met his initial goal, / but he knew / he had made something / other people would want.

7. When Ruth took the cookies / out of the oven, / she got a surprise.

8. A baker's mistake / became a milestone / in the history of cookies.

Invented by Mistake

Read the sentences and circle the words that have the /o͝o/ sound you hear in
hook. **Then follow the directions.**

1. The man is a very good cook. Put a cook's hat on his head.
2. The cook made a cooking fire. Draw the flames.
3. The cook keeps extra wood in the bucket. Put some wood in the bucket.
4. The cookbook is on the counter. Draw a picture to go with the cooking directions.
5. Look for the broken dish. Add the part that is missing.
6. The cook shook salt and pepper into the food. Draw dots to show the salt and pepper grains.
7. Should the cook add more salt, or more pepper? Write "S" or "P" on the shaker to show which one you would like him to add.
8. The cook took some meat out of the freezer. Draw the meat on a plate.
9. The cook is using a crooked spoon. Draw a spoon with a handle that is not crooked, and put it on the counter.
10. The cook should not overlook the time. Draw a clock or timer for him to use.
11. There should be more books on the bookshelf. Add some.
12. The cook made some cookies earlier. Draw cookies on the cookie sheet.

Invented by Mistake

Write one sentence in each box below to show what you learned in "Invented by Mistake."

Page 142

Main Idea:

Page 143

Main Idea:

Page 144

Main Idea:

Page 145

Main Idea:

Page 146

Main Idea:

Page 147

Main Idea:

Now write a one sentence summary statement about the selection.

_____

_____

Harcourt

Text Structure: Compare and Contrast

Read the paragraphs.

Have you ever wanted a cup of hot cocoa on a cold winter's day? You might just have poured some cocoa mix into a cup with a little water or milk and popped it in the microwave. Of course, you had to decide which power setting to use, and how long to heat the cocoa. To check whether the mixture was warm enough, you probably stuck your finger in it.

What would you have done one hundred years ago to heat up that cup of cocoa? Well, first of all you would have put wood, or another source of fuel such as coal, in the stove. You would have lit it and waited while the stove heated up. Then you would have put milk, sugar, and a small piece of solid chocolate into a small pan on the stovetop. You probably would have tested the temperature of the milk by sticking your finger in it to see if it was just right.

➡ **Complete the chart to compare and contrast making a cup of cocoa.**

Cup of Cocoa

100 Years Ago	Today

Use the information in the chart to answer these questions.

1. In what way is making a cup of cocoa today similar to making one 100 years ago?

_____

_____

2. Which method of making a cup of cocoa would you prefer and why?

_____

_____

_____

Harcourt

Fluency Builder

realistic	through	Rudy
miniature	started	drew
dependent	picture	cruised
three-dimensional	paper	stooped
recognition	teacher	blue
represented	how	school
		chew
		Tuesday

1. Rudy and Brent cruised / through the middle school crowd / and started for home.

2. The picture you drew / of a bulldog / is so realistic / it looks as if the dog / will chew up the paper.

3. "Your winning, / however, / is dependent / on your finishing / by Tuesday," / said the homeroom teacher.

4. He stooped down / to pet the small dog, / and the pooch remained underfoot.

5. He looks / as if he might be / a miniature collie.

6. He added / some delicate blue shading / for a three-dimensional look.

7. I'm amazed / at how perfectly / you represented / his markings / in your drawing.

8. That kind / of recognition / equals a blue ribbon.

Honorable Mention

Circle and write the word that best completes each sentence.

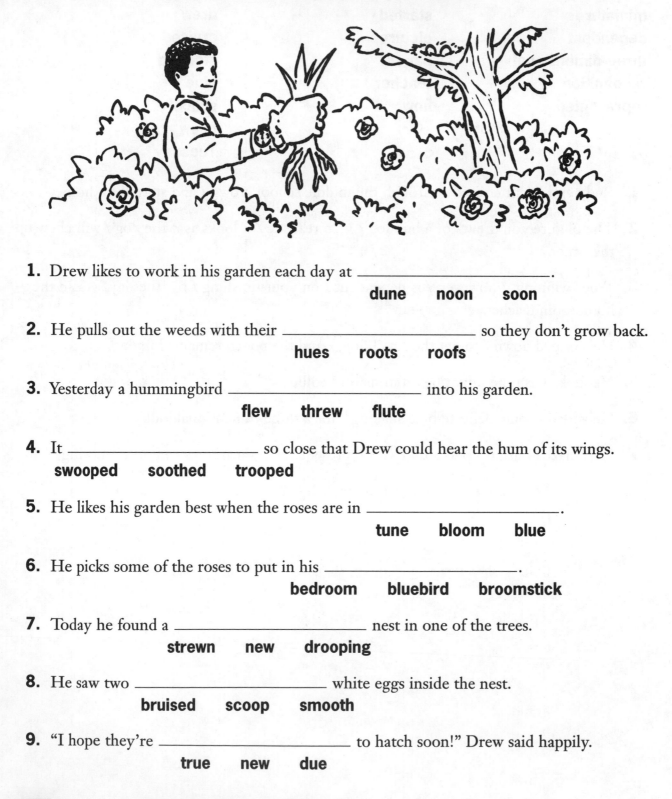

1. Drew likes to work in his garden each day at _____.

   dune   noon   soon

2. He pulls out the weeds with their _____ so they don't grow back.

   hues   roots   roofs

3. Yesterday a hummingbird _____ into his garden.

   flew   threw   flute

4. It _____ so close that Drew could hear the hum of its wings.

   swooped   soothed   trooped

5. He likes his garden best when the roses are in _____.

   tune   bloom   blue

6. He picks some of the roses to put in his _____.

   bedroom   bluebird   broomstick

7. Today he found a _____ nest in one of the trees.

   strewn   new   drooping

8. He saw two _____ white eggs inside the nest.

   bruised   scoop   smooth

9. "I hope they're _____ to hatch soon!" Drew said happily.

   true   new   due

Name _____

Honorable Mention

Complete the story map below to help you summarize "Honorable Mention."
Be sure to write the events in the correct order.

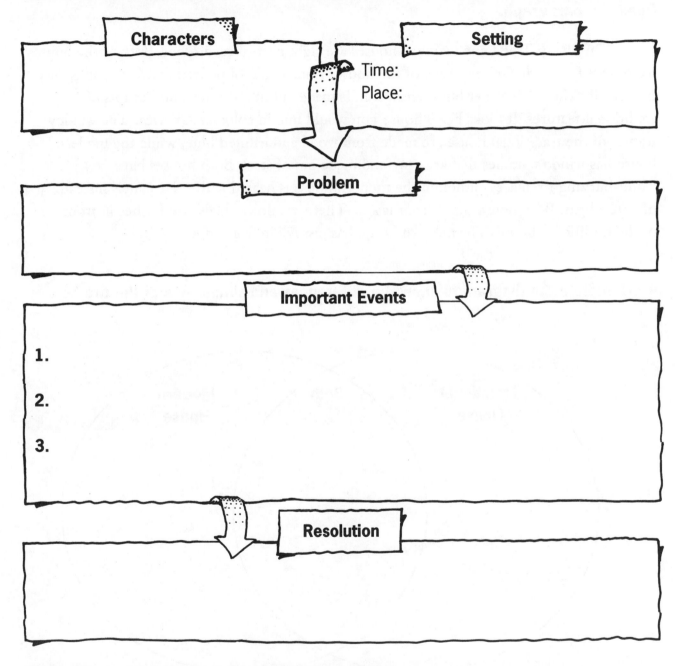

Characters

Setting

Time:
Place:

Problem

Important Events

1.

2.

3.

Resolution

Now write a one-sentence summary of the story.

_____

_____

Name _____

Text Structure: Compare and Contrast

Read the paragraph.

On Shady Tree Lane two new houses are right next to each other. Both of the houses were built for single families. One of the houses is made out of poured concrete and is very modern looking. The other house, however, is made out of red brick and has lots of traditional features. It looks like a house you would find in colonial America. The window frames of the traditional house are made from wood and painted blue, while the modern house has window frames that are gray and made out of steel. Both houses have wood-burning fireplaces, although the modern house is heated with solar panels instead of natural gas. Both houses have front lawns. There are flower beds and bushes in front of the traditional house. The modern house has just ivy in front of it.

➡ **Complete the diagram to show the differences and similarities of the two houses.**

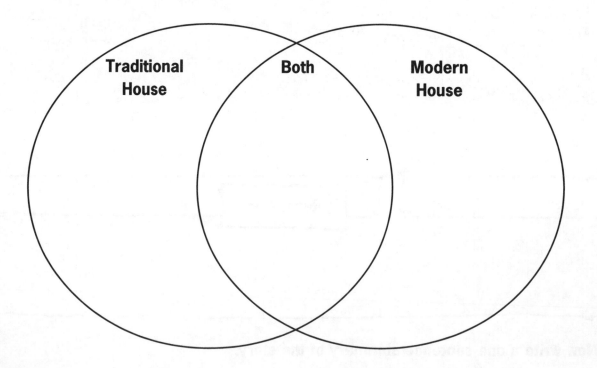

Harcourt

Fluency Builder

rugged	knew	unwrapped
forge	pound	knack
tributes	really	gnawed
ornamental	made	knees
install	not	written
portable	everything	knocked
	words	
	letters	

1. A 2,080 pound bell / is not really portable, / and when it was unwrapped / and tested, / it cracked.

2. Pennsylvania's leaders / were not willing / to install a cracked bell, / so two strong, / rugged men / broke up the bell.

3. John Stow had a knack / for working with metal. / At his forge, / he made everything / from ornamental candlesticks / to ordinary tools.

4. John Stow knew / he would need help, / but not much is known / about his assistant, / John Pass.

5. As he waited / for the test, / worry gnawed at him, / and his knees trembled.

6. The bell made an ugly clank / like the sound of two shovels / being knocked together.

7. People paid many tributes / to the two ordinary workers / who had created an extraordinary bell.

8. Written in large letters / on the Liberty Bell / are the words / *Pass and Stow*.

Harcourt

Making Freedom's Bell

Read the story. Circle all the words in which the /n/ sound is spelled *gn* or *kn*. Draw a line under words in which the /r/ sound is spelled *wr*.

Ken was riding up a grassy knoll on his bike. Another biker was riding down the knoll—on the wrong side of the trail. The two bikers got in a wreck. Ken's knapsack went flying. The other biker hurt her kneecap. She had hit her knee on a big gnarled tree. Ken felt angry. "Thanks to you, my bike is wrecked and my wrist hurts," he said. "Let me write your name down."

"Sorry about your wrist. I'll wrap it for you. I can fix your bike. I have a real knack for repairs," said the other biker as she got out a wrench.

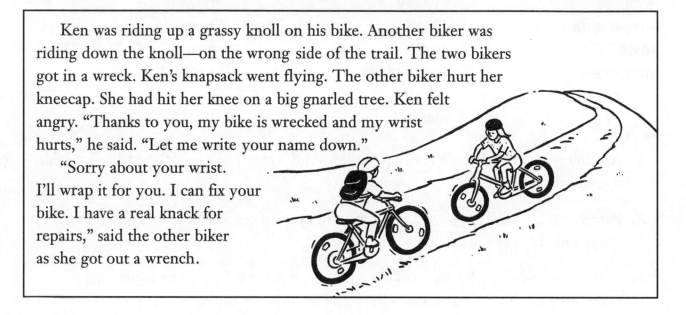

Circle and write the word that best completes each sentence.

1. Ken rode up a _____ on his bike.

          knoll   **know**   **note**

2. Another biker came down going the

_____ way.

          wrote   **wrong**   **rung**

3. A _____ happened when the two bikers crashed into each other.

          wrack   **rack**   **wreck**

4. Ken said he wanted to _____ down the biker's name.

          wrong   **write**   **wrap**

5. He said, "My bike is _____."

          wrestle   **wrecked**   **worn**

6. The other biker got out a _____ to fix Ken's bike.

          wrench   **wren**   **ranch**

7. She said she had a _____ for repairs.

          gnat   **knack**   **kick**

Harcourt

Making Freedom's Bell

Write one or two sentences in each box to tell about the importance of the State House bell.

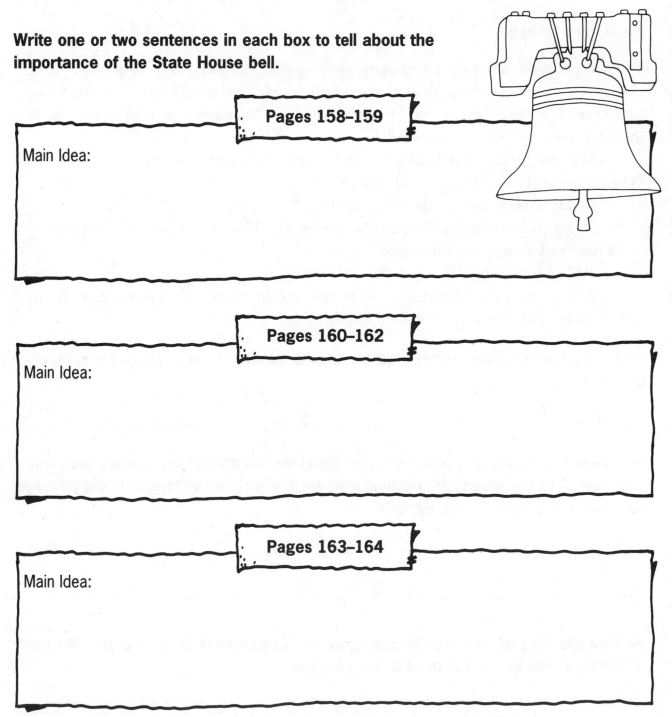

Pages 158–159

Main Idea:

Pages 160–162

Main Idea:

Pages 163–164

Main Idea:

Now write a one-sentence summary statement about the selection.

Word Relationships

Read the passage.

Cleaning up after my sister's party was a big job. The party was fun, but there were blue streamers and wrapping paper all over the floor. My little sister's favorite present was a teddy bear. I had to collect all the refuse from the floor. My mother decided that my brother should go outside. "You need to wind down from all this excitement."

My little brother Teddy said, "It's just as well. I refuse to help you now anyway." When he opened the door, the wind blew in.

I said, "Please close the door!"

Teddy shut the door and my mother remarked, "That was a close one; the garbage could have ended up on the floor again."

"What did you say?" I asked. "I couldn't hear you."

After a while, my little brother threw open the door and said, "I now present the most incredible little brother ever. I am here to help clean."

➡ **Find a homophone—a word that sounds the same—in the passage for each of these words.**

1. blue _____   **2.** here _____

➡ **The words _Teddy_ and _teddy_ are homographs—words that are spelled the same but have different meanings. Homographs may also sound different. In the passage, find four more pairs of homographs.**

1. _____   **3.** _____

2. _____   **4.** _____

➡ **One meaning of _refuse_ is "to not agree to." Use context clues to define the other meaning of _refuse_, as it is used in the passage.**

Clues: _____

_____

Meaning: _____

Harcourt

Fluency Builder

uncertainly	bike	photography
bustled	said	laughed
propelled	find	coughing
elective	down	pharmacy
scowled	little	
sheepishly	myself	
conviction	looked	
	were	
	taking	

1. "Oh, / I'm sure I can find / Grant Avenue," / I said with conviction.

2. Shoppers were bustling / up and down / Main Street.

3. Outside the pharmacy, / I scowled / as I jumped on my bike.

4. I'm taking photography / for an elective.

5. We laughed / and had / a great time.

6. "Yes, / Dad," / I said / a little sheepishly.

7. I smiled and hummed / as I propelled myself / toward Grant Avenue.

8. He looked / at me, / coughing uncertainly.

A Summer Treat

Write the word that answers each riddle.

1. I have the same beginning sound and letters as *phase*.

   You talk into me. What am I? _____

   graph   pencil   phone

2. I have the same ending sound and letters as *enough*.

   I am something you might do after hearing a joke.

   What am I? _____

   sniff   laugh   chuckle

3. I have the same beginning sound and letters as *phase*.

   I am a place that sells medicine. What am I? _____

   pharmacy   drugstore   farm

4. I have the *f* sound spelled *ph*.

   I am a large animal. What am I? _____

   giraffe   panther   elephant

5. I have the same beginning sound and letters as *phony*.

   You take me with a camera. What am I? _____

   picture   photograph   film

6. I have the *f* sound spelled *gh*.

   I describe the way sandpaper feels. What am I? _____

   rough   soft   smooth

7. I have the *f* sound spelled *ph*.

   I am made up of letters. What am I? _____

   book   photograph   alphabet

8. I have the *f* sound spelled *ph*.

   I am the air surrounding our planet. What am I? _____

   autograph   atmosphere   space

9. I have the same ending sound and letters as *laugh*.

   I mean the same as *plenty*. What am I? _____

   full   enough   many

Name _____

A Summer Treat

Complete the sequence chart for "A Summer Treat." Write a sentence in each box. The first box has been completed for you.

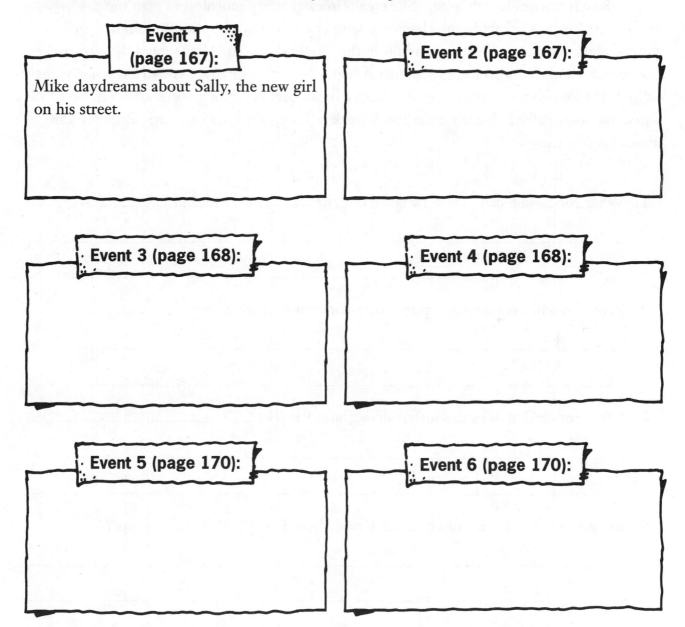

Event 1 (page 167):
Mike daydreams about Sally, the new girl on his street.

Event 2 (page 167):

Event 3 (page 168):

Event 4 (page 168):

Event 5 (page 170):

Event 6 (page 170):

Now use the information from the boxes to write a one-sentence summary of the selection.

_____

_____

Harcourt

Draw Conclusions

Read the paragraph below. Then answer the questions that follow.

Karen teaches fourth grade. She comes in early every morning to plan the day's lessons. At lunch, she eats in the classroom with any students who want to join her, even though most teachers eat with the adults in the Teacher's Room. After school, Karen coaches the speech team. She also tutors students at night. Her friend Patrick is also a teacher at the school. He told Karen that she needs to take a break because she's getting worn out by all the work she does. Patrick doesn't do as much work as Karen does, so he clearly does not care about his students.

1. What conclusion can you draw about Karen? _____

_____

_____

2. What evidence is there to support your conclusion about Karen? _____

_____

_____

3. What conclusion does the author draw about Patrick? _____

_____

_____

4. Do you agree with the author's conclusion about Patrick? Why or why not?

_____

_____

Harcourt

Fluency Builder

tentative	tried	Heather
muster	said	pleasant
appreciatively	would	heavy
gestured	smile	breath
mystified	after	healthy
significance	words	ahead
	bread	threatened

1. I took a deep breath, / tried to muster a smile, / and said, "I'll do it!"

2. Dad quietly gestured / that he would / go ahead of us / with my heavy bags.

3. Now, / with a healthy helper like you, / I no longer feel threatened.

4. Grandma's words / had significance / for me.

5. Mom and Dad / made tentative plans / for helping out Grandma.

6. I was totally mystified / about the bread.

7. My mother and father / smiled back / appreciatively.

8. After my chores / I read outdoors / in the pleasant weather.

Name _____

Heather's Farm Summer

Fill in the letter in front of the sentence that tells about the picture.

1. (A) Edna likes to be well-read.
   (B) Edna likes to melt lead.
   (C) Edna likes to find feathers.
   (D) Edna likes to bake bread.

2. (F) Tom spreads his shirt on the floor.
   (G) Tom heads for the shirt shop.
   (H) Tom threads a needle to fix his shirt.
   (J) Tom dreads cleaning his shirt.

3. (A) Glenda sees that the weather is nice.
   (B) Glenda sees a feather on the street.
   (C) Glenda sees that the box is too heavy.
   (D) Glenda sees that her mom is not ready.

4. (F) After running, Eric is wealthy.
   (G) After running, Eric is sweaty and breathless.
   (H) After running, Eric holds his head high.
   (J) After running, Eric snacks on bread.

5. (A) Inspector Jan looked at the loaf of bread.
   (B) Inspector Jan looked at the feathers.
   (C) Inspector Jan looked at the weather.
   (D) Inspector Jan looked at the marks made
       by the tire treads.

6. (F) Mark made a healthful salad.
   (G) Mark made a dinner of bread.
   (H) Mark made a heavy dinner.
   (J) Mark made dinner in the meadow.

7. (A) The mouse has a home in the bread.
   (B) The mouse has a home full of feathers.
   (C) The mouse has a home in the meadow.
   (D) The mouse has a home that is unpleasant.

Heather's Farm Summer

Complete the story map below to help you summarize "Heather's Farm Summer."
Be sure to write the events in the correct order.

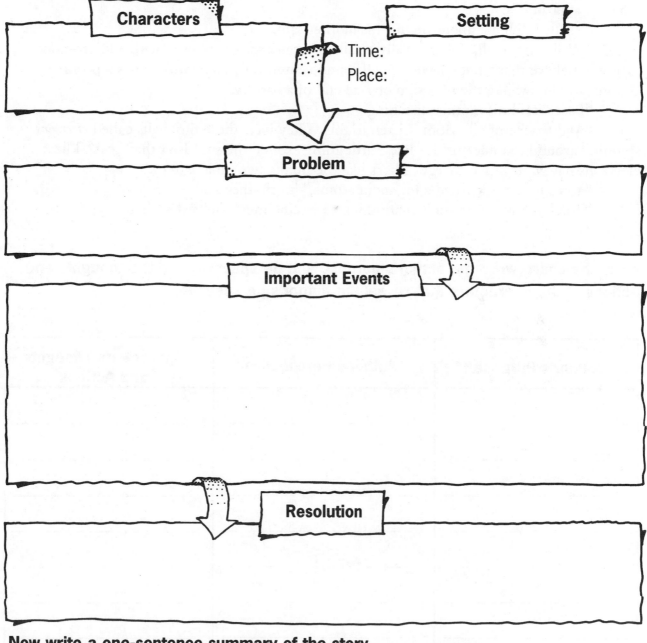

Characters

Setting

Time:

Place:

Problem

Important Events

Resolution

Now write a one-sentence summary of the story.

_____

_____

Harcourt

Author's Purpose and Perspective

Read the passage.

Richard came home from school excited. "Mom," he said, "I just learned about atoms! They're amazing!"

"Really? Tell me about them," his mother said.

"Well, first of all, they're really small. You can't see them, even with a microscope. Can you believe that? They have a small round center, called a *nucleus*. It has a positive charge, you know, like the plus sign on one end of a battery."

"I see," said his mother, listening.

"And that's not all, Mom. Listen to this: They have these tiny balls called *electrons* spinning around the nucleus. It's like Earth going around the sun! Isn't that neat? These electrons have a negative charge. That's like the minus sign on a battery."

"You sure have learned a lot about atoms," his mother said.

"Totally! I've never studied anything so fascinating," Richard replied.

➡ **In the chart, write the author's purpose and perspective, and the thoughts and actions of the characters that reveal the author's perspective.**

Author's Purpose	Author's Perspective	Character's Thoughts and Actions
_____	_____	_____
_____	_____	_____
_____	_____	_____
_____	_____	_____
_____	_____	_____
_____	_____	_____
_____	_____	_____
_____	_____	_____

Harcourt

Fluency Builder

precision	used	freight
devised	paper	outweighed
gradually	dog	eighteen
dormitory	two	break
transcribe	them	great
stylus	who	
	stay	
	news	
	worked	

1. Morris Frank was blind, / but he used a stylus / and paper / to transcribe notes / in Braille.

2. Frank traveled / as freight / to Switzerland.

3. As the man / and dog trained together, / the signals gradually / became obvious to him.

4. The dog's trainer / had devised a way / for Frank to feel / her movements.

5. The two / of them worked / together / with great precision.

6. Reporters / looking for a news break / wanted to put them / to a test.

7. The benefits / to others / outweighed the risks, / and it took only eighteen / to twenty seconds / to cross the busy street.

8. People who are blind / stay in a dormitory / at The Seeing Eye / training center / while they learn / to handle / their dog.

A Friend in Need

Read the story. Circle the words that have the /ā/ sound spelled *ea*, *ei*, or *eigh*.

Dana is eighteen years old. She lives in Wisconsin, just a few miles south of Lake Superior, one of the Great Lakes. Another smaller lake is only about a mile away from her house.

Dana always says that lakes are a big part of her life. She likes to go to Lake Superior to watch the great ships go by. Some of the ships weigh thousands of tons. Dana likes to pretend that she is a passenger on a freight ship on its way to a distant country. She wonders how much she would add to the ship's weight. Probably not much!

Dana also likes to go fishing in the small lake near her house. At daybreak she pushes out in her rowboat. Her neighbor Fay often goes with her. The girls usually get back by eight o'clock in the morning. On a good day they have fish steaks for dinner.

Now write a word that you circled in the story to complete each sentence.

1. Dana lives close to one of the _____ Lakes.

2. She is _____ years old.

3. She likes to watch the _____ ships go by on Lake Superior.

4. She also likes to fish with her _____.

5. Sometimes Dana pretends that she is a passenger on a _____ ship.

6. A ship can _____ thousands of tons.

7. She doesn't think she would add much to its _____.

8. Dana leaves her house at _____ to go fishing.

9. Dana usually gets back from her fishing trips by _____.

Harcourt

A Friend in Need

Name_____

Complete the sequence chart about "A Friend in Need." Write a sentence in each box. The first box has been completed for you.

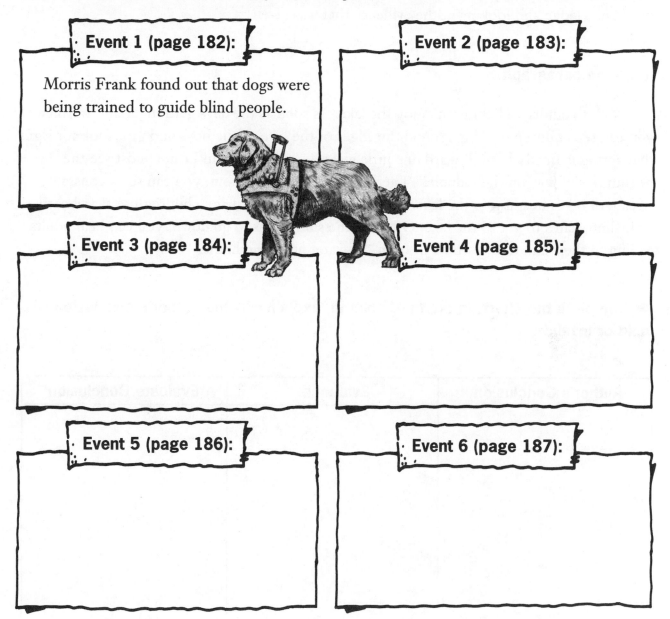

Event 1 (page 182):

Morris Frank found out that dogs were being trained to guide blind people.

Event 2 (page 183):

Event 3 (page 184):

Event 4 (page 185):

Event 5 (page 186):

Event 6 (page 187):

Now use the information from the boxes to write a one-sentence summary of the selection.

_____

_____

Draw Conclusions

When you draw conclusions, you use evidence in the text and your own knowledge. Valid conclusions can be supported by evidence. Evaluating an author's conclusions includes using your knowledge and looking at the evidence that was given.

Read the paragraph.

  Both adults and children enjoy the lake. As soon as the days get longer and warmer, you can see children walking around the edges of the lake. Little boys and girls look for signs that spring is finally here. I heard one little girl say, "Oh my gosh! I can almost see the beginnings of legs on the tadpole!" Then, as soon as school is out, you can see a constant stream of bikes heading to the lake. You will also notice that many children use skateboards or in-line skates to get to the lake. Often, as the sun begins to go down, you can hear adults calling to their children to come in from the water and head home.

➡️ **Complete the chart. In the third column, explain why the author's conclusion is valid or invalid.**

Author's Conclusion	Evidence	Evaluate Conclusion

Harcourt

Fluency Builder

dramatically	get	through
solemnly	me	enough
irresistible	into	thought
sublime	came	though
fluster	here	tough
bewildered	how	brought
	laughed	
	couldn't	

1. "Don't get me / into / a fluster," said Jim.

2. "We came all the way up here / from 48th Street / for the sublime thrill / of seeing the White Sox / in person," Jim said dramatically.

3. "I'm naughty, / but my charm / is irresistible," laughed Jim.

4. "We have to figure out / how to get you / inside first, / though," Billy said to Susie.

5. "I thought / you South Side boys / were all tough," the worker said to Ben.

6. "He's not going / to let us / through there," Tommy said in a bewildered voice.

7. "We don't have / enough money / for tickets," said Tommy solemnly.

8. "My mother / said I couldn't go / unless I / brought her," Billy said sheepishly.

Sitting It Out

Read the sentences and circle the words that have the letter pattern *ough*. Then follow the directions.

1. The man is going through the express checkout line. Make a sign that says *Express*.
2. The man brought his daughter with him to the store. Draw his daughter next to him.
3. The man bought milk and cereal. Add a milk carton next to the cereal.
4. The man bought a half dozen doughnuts. Draw three more doughnuts to make a half dozen.
5. The man does not have enough money. Draw a few extra dollars in his hand.
6. The man's daughter thinks they ought to buy a magazine. Put a magazine in her hand.
7. Although the man wants to get the magazine, he doesn't have enough money. Draw an X on the magazine.
8. The woman behind the counter thought the man's daughter was well-behaved, so she gave her a treat. Draw the treat.
9. The man asks the woman to make sure the sacks are tough enough not to break. Draw two paper sacks around the groceries.
10. Because the woman does a thorough job bagging the groceries, the man gives her a tip. Draw a few coins on the counter.

Harcourt

Name _____

Sitting It Out

Complete the story map below to help you summarize "Sitting It Out."
Be sure to write the events in correct order.

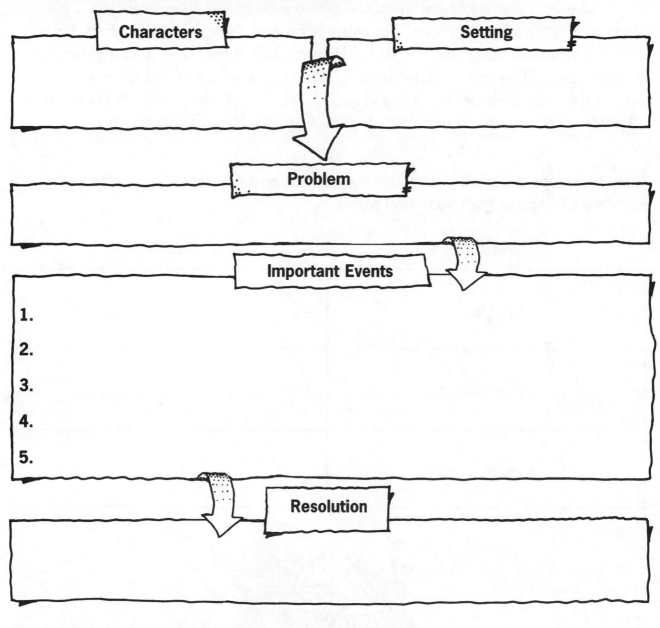

Characters

Setting

Problem

Important Events

1.

2.

3.

4.

5.

Resolution

Now write one or two sentences to summarize the story.

_____

_____

_____

Name _____

Word Relationships

Read the paragraph, paying attention to the underlined words.

    I recently moved to a new town. Our next-door neighbors have three boys. I was happy to have friends to play with. The oldest boy is Dan. I like how <u>affable</u> he is. He is always in a good mood and easy to talk to. The next child in the family is Maury. Boy, is he <u>pugnacious</u>! He is very quick to argue and gets angry a lot. He often challenges me to fight about the things we're arguing about. The youngest of the children is Wally, the <u>idler</u>. He never wants to do anything! He just sits around. He's kind of annoying.

Now, complete the chart below. Use the context of the paragraph to write the meaning of each of the underlined words.

Word	Meaning
affable	_____
pugnacious	_____
idler	_____

Harcourt

Fluency Builder

compliant	everyone	listen
permeate	through	whistling
corralled	little	climb
full-fledged	very	solemn
diversion	smell	herbs
craggy	your	thistles
ornery		honest

1. Listen, / we've got what you need / to be a full-fledged cowboy.

2. Why, / you'd be plumb ornery / with an icy breeze / whistling up your pant legs!

3. Folks do say / the smell / of an old Stetson / can permeate a room.

4. Red will make / even the calmest / and most solemn cows / ornery.

5. In our shirts / you'll have cattle / that are tranquil / and compliant.

6. We know / you ride and climb / over rough, / craggy terrain / twelve hours a day, / through thistles / and thorny herbs.

7. Honest, / you'll look good in the saddle / until the very last cow / is corralled / at the end of the trail.

8. Everyone needs / a little diversion / and fun / during these evenings / by the campfire.

The Cowboy's Catalog

Read the story. Circle the words that have *b*, *h*, *t*, or *n* as a silent letter.

Zeke got up and combed his hair. He made toast and wiped up the crumbs. After breakfast, he walked to the library. As he walked, he whistled. When he got inside the library, he approached the solemn librarian. She listened as Zeke explained that his book was overdue. He handed her the book about mountain climbing. She checked the columns on her computer screen. Her stern face softened into a smile as she looked back at Zeke. "That was very honest of you," she told him. She pushed a button on her keyboard with her thumb. "Because you acted honorably, I'll erase your fine," she told Zeke.

Answer the questions about the story using complete sentences. Include one of the words you circled in each answer.

1. What did Zeke do while he walked? _____

_____

2. What was Zeke's book about? _____

_____

3. What does the librarian check on her computer screen? _____

_____

4. Why does the librarian erase Zeke's fine? _____

_____

Harcourt

The Cowboy's Catalog

Write one or two sentences in each box below to show what cowboys can order from "The Cowboy's Catalog."

Page 200

What does the catalog sell to keep cowboys warm?

Page 201

Tell what cowboys can buy for their heads.

Page 202

Describe the shirts and pants sold in the Cowboy's Catalog.

Pages 203–204

What three special items do all cowboys need?

Now write a one-sentence summary of the selection.

_____

_____

Harcourt

Author's Purpose and Perspective

Read the paragraph.

      Architecture is a combination of art, science, and math. Students in high school who would like to be architects should take as many of those courses as they can. Architecture students in college must learn how buildings are designed and built. They need to know how to make models from drawings. They also have to spend many hours learning to draw and design on the computer. After finishing school, they will work in an architecture firm. Then they will need to study some more to take special tests so they can be full-fledged architects.

➡ **Complete the diagram by listing the details and then stating the author's perspective.**

Details
_____
_____
_____
_____

↓

Author's Perspective
_____
_____
_____
_____

Harcourt

Fluency Builder

submerged   some   disconnected
cylinder   inside   researchers
transparent   countries   returning
microscopic   many   unable
collide   have   disbelief
traditional   were   unexpectedly
                    one
                    rock

1. In some countries, / volcanic eruptions / have submerged / entire islands.

2. Roads and highways / broke up / and disconnected, / causing cars to collide.

3. Many people / were returning home / and were unable to escape / from the collapsing roads.

4. However, / researchers are studying / every microscopic movement / of the earth / to learn more.

5. The traditional image / of an active volcano / is of one / on a faraway / tropical island.

6. Molten rock / and hot ash / rushed up the cylinder-shaped shaft inside / and shot to the surface.

7. A transparent veil / of smoke / had risen from the top / of the mountain.

8. The unaware / and unprepared people /reacted in disbelief / as the unannounced / earthquake unexpectedly struck.

Harcourt

Name _____

Great Shakes!

Read the story. Circle the words that have one of the following prefixes: *un-*, *re-*, *dis-*.

Marty was unhappy with the mess in his room. He had never seen the room look so untidy. His favorite music tape had disappeared. His bed was unmade. Even his shoes were disorganized. Marty decided to reorganize all his things.

First he reordered his books and tapes. Then he remade his bed. The room looked great, but Marty was still dissatisfied. He had been unable to find his favorite music tape. He decided to retrace his steps. Last night he had listened to the tape after dinner. When it was done he had rewound it and placed it back on the shelf. Or had he? Marty reopened his tape player. He stared at it in disbelief. There was the tape! It had been there all along!

Now write the word with a prefix from above that best completes each sentence.

1. Marty thought his room looked _____.

2. His bed was _____ and his books were unshelved.

3. His shoes were all _____.

4. One of his music tapes had _____.

5. He decided he would _____ his things.

6. Marty _____ the books and tapes.

7. He was still _____ to find the music tape.

8. To find the tape, Marty decided to _____ his steps.

9. He found it when he _____ the tape player.

Harcourt

Name

Great Shakes!

Complete the cause-and-effect chart to help you summarize "Great Shakes!"

CAUSE:	CAUSE:	CAUSE:
San Francisco Earthquake 1906	Mount Saint Helens's Eruption 1980	San Francisco Earthquake, 1989
EFFECTS:	**EFFECTS:**	**EFFECTS:**
_____	_____	_____
_____	_____	_____
_____	_____	_____
_____	_____	_____
_____	_____	_____
_____	_____	_____
_____	_____	_____
_____	_____	_____

Now use the information in the boxes to summarize how earthquakes and volcanoes have affected the North American continent.

_____

_____

_____

_____

Harcourt

Name _____

Text Structure: Cause and Effect

Read the paragraph.

The French Revolution of 1789 had many causes. France had been a powerful nation in Europe. However, as its population grew, many poor people did not have enough to eat. These poor people grew their own food, but had to pay rent to the people who owned the land on which they grew the food. This caused the poor to have bad feelings toward the wealthy landowners. The wealthy landowners were unhappy because the French kings were becoming too powerful. This also made the clergy of the Roman Catholic Church unhappy. In addition, the poor disliked the French kings and blamed them for the rising prices.

➡ **Complete the diagram.**

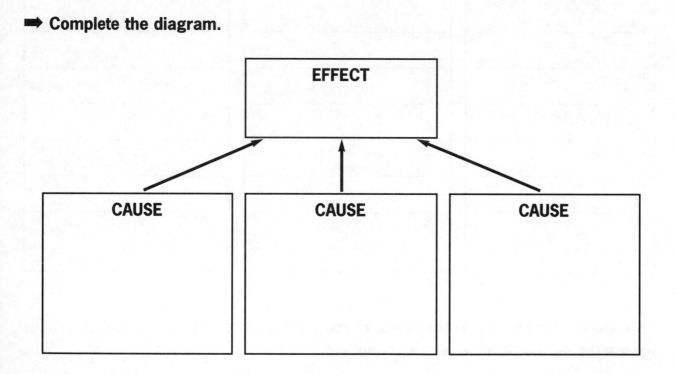

Harcourt

Fluency Builder

abounded	after	loudly
buoyancy	knew	seemingly
dissipated	happy	fully
diversity	fully	heartless
acoustic	first	harmless
gauge	sign	
salvage	any	
	board	

1. Excitement abounded / among the passengers and crew / on board.

2. At first, / passengers disregarded / the seemingly harmless incident.

3. Even with the diversity / of video and acoustic equipment, / they could find no sign / of the *Titanic*.

4. The crew cheered loudly, / knowing they had / at least discovered the wreck.

5. A depth gauge showed / that the *Titanic* was / two and a half miles / beneath the surface.

6. They knew / it would be heartless / to salvage / any of the wreckage.

7. After all, / the ship was said / to have great buoyancy.

8. However, / after the crew / had fully inspected the damage, / the happy mood on board / dissipated.

Finding the Titanic

**Fill in the oval in front of the sentence that
tells about the picture.**

1. ⬭ Tina thinks the bowl is useless.
   ⬭ Tina slowly cleans the bowl.
   ⬭ Tina eats a bowlful of cereal.

2. ⬭ She runs quickly to school.
   ⬭ She walks slowly to the mall.
   ⬭ She runs quickly up the hill.

3. ⬭ It is almost unbearable to wait!
   ⬭ Tina finds today's lessons
     enjoyable.
   ⬭ Tina thinks it is useless to try the
     phone again.

4. ⬭ She leaves the room quickly.
   ⬭ She waits calmly.
   ⬭ She waits nervously.

5. ⬭ Tina starts off softly.
   ⬭ Tina sings loudly.
   ⬭ Tina sings shyly.

6. ⬭ The directors yell angrily at each
     other.
   ⬭ The directors are boastful.
   ⬭ The directors talk quietly after she
     finishes.

7. ⬭ "That was wonderful! You're in the
     musical!"
   ⬭ "I'm doubtful that you'll get
     a part."
   ⬭ "Your audition was unsuccessful."

Harcourt

Name _____

Finding the *Titanic*

Write one or two sentences in each box below to show what you learned about the *Titanic* from reading this selection.

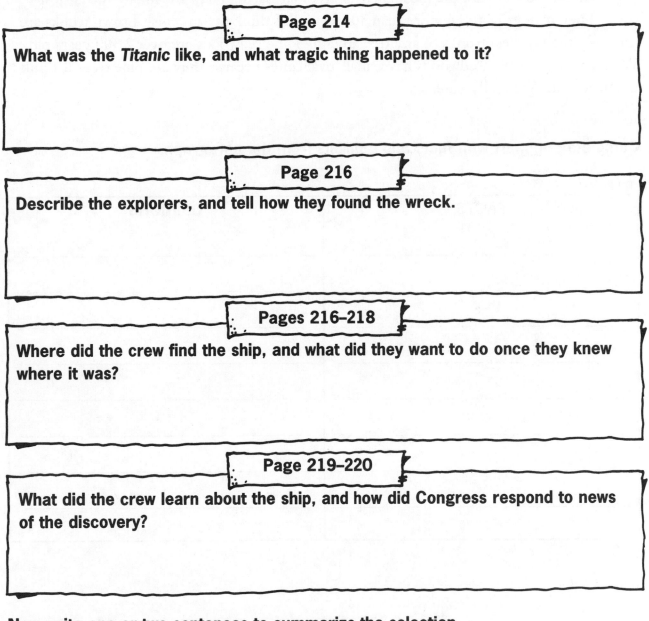

Page 214

What was the *Titanic* like, and what tragic thing happened to it?

Page 216

Describe the explorers, and tell how they found the wreck.

Pages 216–218

Where did the crew find the ship, and what did they want to do once they knew where it was?

Page 219–220

What did the crew learn about the ship, and how did Congress respond to news of the discovery?

Now write one or two sentences to summarize the selection.

_____

_____

_____

Name _____

Fact and Opinion

Read the paragraph below.

    Redwood trees are the most amazing trees on Earth. They are among the largest trees. They may grow to be more than 300 feet tall. I think their reddish-brown trunks are probably the prettiest trunks of any tree around. Some redwoods are over 2,300 years old. What awesome trees! Redwoods have small, oval cones because they are pine trees. I think the little cones are really cute.

Complete the chart with facts and opinions from the paragraph.

FACTS	OPINIONS
_____	_____
_____	_____
_____	_____
_____	_____
_____	_____
_____	_____

Harcourt

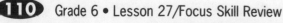

Name _____

Fluency Builder

maneuver	American	impossible
high-tech	found	nonliving
facilities	once	preview
navigation	were	predates
mission	his	
simulation	with	
	our	
	from	
	use	
	would	

1. Russian cosmonaut / Yuri Gagarin's / flight into space / predates the flight / of American astronaut / Alan Shepard.

2. Astronauts / use flight simulation / to prepare / for the weightlessness / of space.

3. Alan Shepard's duties were / to analyze his responses / to the flight, / to maneuver his spacecraft / with high-tech controls, / and to survive.

4. On July 16, / 1969, / *Apollo 11* was launched / from the Kennedy Space Center's facilities.

5. The American space program / turned to navigation / among the planets / of our solar system.

6. NASA scientists / found only nonliving materials / on Mars.

7. Scientists once believed / that it would be impossible / to send humans to Mars.

8. The uncrewed / *Voyager* missions / were designed to preview / and explore / the outer planets.

Harcourt

Mission Possible

Circle and write the word that answers each riddle.

1. I mean "pass out of sight."

Which word am I? _____

      disease   **disappear**   **displease**

2. I mean "a look at something beforehand."

Which word am I? _____

      predate   **predict**   **preview**

3. I mean "rude."

Which word am I? _____

      impolite   **imperfect**   **immune**

4. I tell what you do if you fix a sand castle that has fallen down.

Which word am I? _____

      remind   **remake**   **remark**

5. I mean "not alive."

Which word am I? _____

      nonliving   **nonsense**   **nonfat**

6. I name something that can't be done.

Which word am I? _____

      impossible   **impassable**   **important**

7. I mean "sad."

Which word am I? _____

      underneath   **underway**   **unhappy**

8. I mean "consider one more time."

Which word am I? _____

      rethink   **rewind**   **redo**

9. I describe someone who never says "Thanks."

Which word am I? _____

      unhappy   **undeserved**   **ungrateful**

Harcourt

Mission Possible

You are about to read a story titled "Mission Possible." Read the story fact sheet.

Date:	Who or What:	What Happened:
April 12, 1961	Soviet cosmonaut Yuri Gagarin	Gagarin was the first person in space.
May 5, 1961	American **astronaut** Alan Shepard	Shepard was the first American in space. During his trip he was in a state of **weightlessness**. This was because he was far away from Earth. Earth's **gravity** did not affect him.
1975–1976	*Viking* **orbiters**	The orbiters went to Mars. They sent down landers to collect soil. The planet's soil was **analyzed** in a lab. **Specialists** wanted to find out if there was life on Mars.

Now answer these questions in complete sentences. Use each word in dark type from the fact sheet one time.

1. What went to Mars? _____

2. What happened to the soil that was collected on Mars? _____

_____

3. What did the specialists want to find out? _____

_____

4. Who is Alan Shepard? _____

5. Because Shepard was far from Earth, what did not affect him? _____

_____

6. What state was Shepard in during his trip? _____

_____

Text Structure: Cause and Effect

Read the paragraph below. Look for cause-and-effect relationships.

In western states like Montana and Oregon, many people camp in the forests and on the mountains. Bears live in these areas. Some campers leave food and garbage lying around their campsites. The bears have a very good sense of smell and go to these campsites to eat the food they smell. This often puts them in contact with humans. A frightened human may decide to shoot a bear, or a bear may get frightened and attack a human. Over time, bears may lose their natural fear of humans and start to go to where people are. This is dangerous for both people and bears.

➡️ **Complete the chart.**

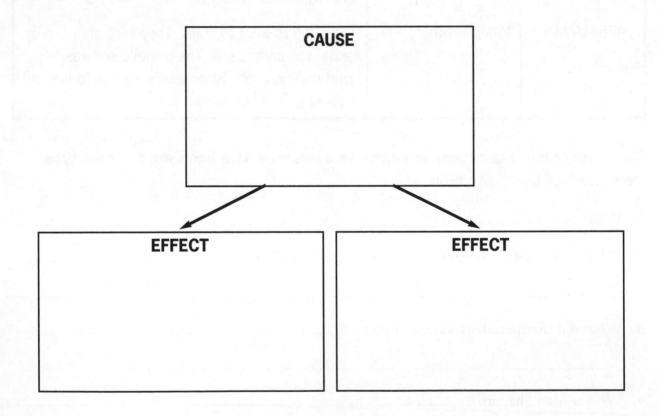

Harcourt

Fluency Builder

bombarded	your	information
modem	sometimes	permission
interactive	get	donation
transmission	find	destination
online	make	decision
barrage	friend	collection
	with	question

1. The transmission / of the files is handled / by your computer modem.

2. The modem is a piece / of interactive equipment / that lets your computer communicate / with other computers.

3. To answer a question / about astronauts, / hop online / and go to the Air and Space Museum's Web site.

4. A popular Web site / sometimes will get bombarded / with "hits."

5. The barrage / of signals can mean / a delay for you.

6. This browser can find / a destination with / an amazing collection / of information.

7. Before / you make the decision / to go online, / get permission / from an adult you trust.

8. Can you make / a donation of your time / to send an e-mail / for a friend?

Untangling the Web

Read the story. Circle all the words that end with *-tion*, *-sion*, or *-ion*.

Eric felt a sense of elation as he boarded the plane with his family. Finally they were going on vacation! When he got to his seat, he found a comfortable position. He buried his nose in a nonfiction book about famous inventions.

"Eric, where are your glasses?" his father asked sternly. "You know it's bad for your vision to read without them."

"I know, I know," sighed Eric. "You've told me so a million times." He fished his glasses out of his backpack and put them on. The small print in the captions of his book suddenly became very clear. Still, he thought the glasses looked silly.

Soon, the flight attendant brought their lunches. "You have two options," she told Eric, "roast beef with onions or chicken with peas."

"That's a tough decision!" said Eric. "I guess I'll take the roast beef."

"That's a good choice, in my opinion," said the flight attendant. "And by the way," she told Eric, "I want to mention that those glasses make you look quite smart."

"Thanks!" said Eric. That was all the persuasion he needed to keep them on!

Now write a word that you circled in the story to complete each sentence.

1. Eric is happy to be going on _____.

2. He finds a comfortable _____ and starts to read.

3. Eric's father reminds him that wearing his glasses is good for his _____.

4. He has to admit they help him see the _____ more clearly.

5. The flight attendant offers two _____ for lunch.

6. Then she _____ that she thinks his glasses make him look smart.

7. That's all the _____ Eric needs to keep them on!

Name _____

Untangling the Web

**Write one or two sentences in each box below to
show what Newbie learned about the World
Wide Web in "Untangling the Web."**

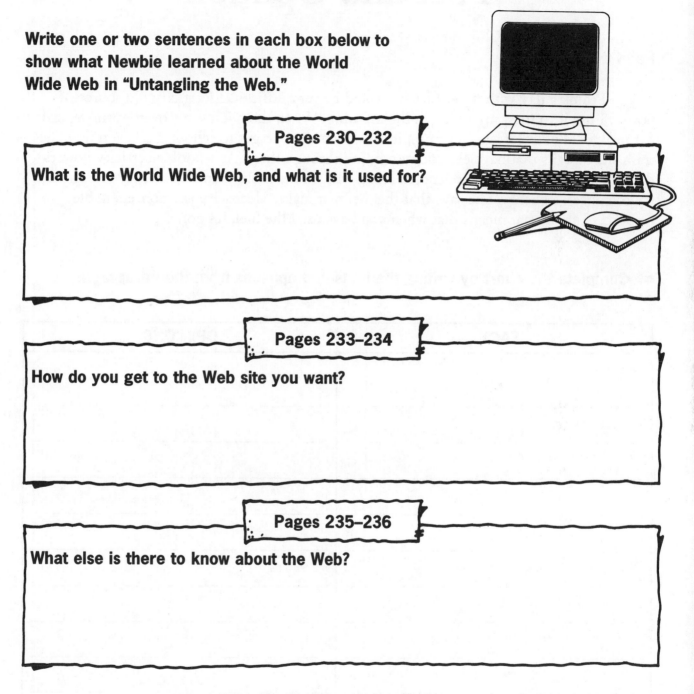

> **Pages 230–232**

What is the World Wide Web, and what is it used for?

> **Pages 233–234**

How do you get to the Web site you want?

> **Pages 235–236**

What else is there to know about the Web?

Write one or two sentences to summarize the selection.

_____

_____

_____

Fact and Opinion

Read the paragraph.

    I think a day without electricity would be very difficult. Electricity is a source of power. I use it to toast my bread in the morning. When the microwave oven warms up my oatmeal (cold oatmeal is disgusting), it uses electricity. To get to school, I take a train. The train sits on rails that have electricity running through them. At school, electricity powers the lights and the bells. My science teacher, who knows more than anyone, says we should try to conserve energy. She says that the fuel that makes electricity is a nonrenewable resource. I think that means that when you have used the fuel, it's gone.

➡ **Complete the chart by writing the facts and opinions from the paragraph.**

FACTS	OPINIONS

Harcourt

Fluency Builder

cosmonaut	found	summer
breakthrough	really	planning
enrolls	plant	came
disregarded	through	Venus
formulas		research
altimeter		atmosphere
satellite		eight
dejectedly		Gene

1. This man / was really a / cosmonaut!

2. The experts / disregarded / my formulas / in planning our flight.

3. He came to see Mars, / the red planet; / Jupiter, / with its rings; / and Venus, with its Great Red Spot.

4. I found / a super Web site / for my research / on plant cells in space.

5. She enrolls / in Space Camp / every summer.

6. I was just talking / about the breakthrough / I made for space science / back in 1969.

7. As our craft rose / through the atmosphere, / we watched the altimeter rise / to eight thousand feet.

8. Gene / sighed / dejectedly.

Harcourt

Cindy "Science" Spots the Clues

Read the sentences and follow the directions. Then draw a line to divide the syllables in the words in dark type. The first sentence has been done for you.

1. This **pic|ture** shows a **ro|bot fac|to|ry**. Make a sign that says "Robot Factory" for the wall.

2. Each worker must wear a **helmet** for **safety**. Put a hard hat on each worker's head.

3. Workers must also wear safety **goggles**. Give each worker safety goggles.

4. The robots **coming** off the assembly line need arms. Add arms to the robots.

5. Find the robot that is also **missing** a leg. Give this robot a leg.

6. The workers listen to **music** as they work. Draw musical notes coming out of the speakers.

7. The man on the left is **testing** how fast each robot can run. Write a number in the display to show how fast this robot is **running**.

8. The man in the **middle washes** off used robot parts. Give him a **washcloth** and **bucket.**

9. The **woman** in the office is **drawing** a new kind of robot. Draw this new kind of robot.

10. On the walls are an **analog** clock and a digital clock. On the digital clock, write the time the **current** school day will be over.

Harcourt

Cindy "Science" Spots the Clues

Complete the sequence chart about "Cindy 'Science' Spots the Clues." Write a sentence or two in each box. The first box has been completed for you.

Event 1:

Cindy Vincent visits her friend Gene's house. Gene is eager for Cindy to meet a special man who was a cosmonaut who once orbited the sun.

Event 2 (page 241):

_____

_____

Event 3 (page 242):

_____

_____

Event 4 (page 243):

_____

_____

_____

Event 5 (page 244):

_____

_____

_____

Now use the information from the boxes to write a one-sentence summary of the selection.

_____

_____

Harcourt

Name _____

Draw Conclusions

Read the paragraphs below. Then complete the charts that follow.

Selection A

    Peter had a cabin in the woods. Each day he would go to the woodpile, load some split logs into his wheelbarrow, and return to the cabin. There, he would stack the logs neatly by the wood stove. He placed the wheelbarrow back in the same spot each day. All of Peter's tools were carefully arranged on his back porch. He swept and mopped the kitchen floor each evening. Before he went to bed, he placed a fresh kettle of water on the stove so that in the morning he could quickly heat it for his coffee.

One Conclusion You Can Draw About Peter	Story Evidence To Support The Conclusion

Selection B

    Darren loves to ride his bike. He rides it very fast, but he always has it under control, and he wears a helmet. He always looks when crossing a street, but he crosses at high speeds. He's never gotten hurt on his bike, but he has almost crashed a few times.

Conclusion	Story Evidence

Harcourt